Praise for *Breakthrou*

"Thanks for a provocative and conceptually rich piece. I enjoyed and got a great deal out of it."

David T. Conley
Professor, University of Oregon
Author, *Who Governs Our Schools?*

"An outstanding book for educators to transform classroom practice and learning strategies. It builds important perspectives on personalizing learning that will inform current practice. Highly recommended."

Brent Davies
Professor, University of Hull (UK)
Author, *The Essentials of School Leadership*

"Fullan, Hill, and Crévola present a model that allows teachers to provide precise instructional strategies to specific students who need timely support in order to master specific skills—without falling victim to the 'prescription trap.' Their critical-pathways concept provides teachers with a powerful framework for integrating preassessment, instructional focus, formative assessment, data analysis, and job-embedded professional development to deliver the precision teaching that leads to continuous improvement. Furthermore, they make a compelling case that this model is not only desirable, but also emminently feasible. Those interested in finding the link between general school-reform initiatives and specific strategies that will actually impact classroom practice will cherish Breakthrough.*"*

Richard DuFour
Educational Consultant
Author, *Professional Learning Communities at Work*

"This is a timely and thought-provoking book. Fullan, Hill, and Crévola address the complexity of teaching and leading, and offer a compelling way forward that focuses on learning for all students through personalization, precision teaching, and professional learning for educators. By connecting assessment with learning, leading with teaching and learning, and classroom instruction with district and government roles and responsibilities, the authors present an

integrated approach that promises to 'break through' the sterile standardization that plagues contemporary education."

Dean Fink
Professor, OISE/University of Toronto
Author, *Leadership for Mortals*

"Breakthrough *is one of those few books that demonstrably understands the importance of personalizing learning and the need to mobilise the whole system towards this goal. Fullan, Hill, and Crévola provide a clear specification of what is required for a learner led curriculum and what it means to work from the classroom out. Their articulation of how assessment leads instruction and is integrated into curriculum design is exemplary."*

David Hopkins
HSBC iNet Chair of International Leadership
Institute of Education, University of London
Author, *Improving The Quality of Education for All*

"Breakthrough *tackles several very thorny problems—how to nurture high-quality classroom instruction on a large scale, and how to do so by building on existing professional know how. Solutions developed in the book warrant careful study by all those with an interest in educational reform."*

Kenneth Leithwood
Professor, OISE/University of Toronto
Author, *Making Schools Smarter*

"Breakthrough *explores interesting possibilities for us to radically individualize classroom instruction—and gives convincing reasons why. I especially like the concept of 'critical pathways' as a way of organizing learning."*

Mike Schmoker
Educational Consultant
Author, *Results: The Key to Continuous School Improvement*

"Breakthrough *points the way to a new definition of effectiveness— one grounded in a powerful theory of action that brings together personalization, precision, and professional learning in new ways. Practical pathways are provided to help the readers apply this theory of action to their own circumstances. Before making any changes, read this book first!"*

Thomas A. Sergiovanni
Lillian Radford Professor of Education
Trinity University (TX)
Author, *Moral Leadership*

"An ambitious and timely manuscript, Breakthrough *is a critical read for those genuinely interested in school reform. Fullan, Hill, and Crévola get to the heart of the matter—improving instruction based on evidence!"*

James Spillane
Olin Professor in Learning and Organization
Northwestern University (IL)
Author, *Distributed Leadership*

*"*Breakthrough *has the potential to make a significant contribution to our thinking in education. The call for personalization of teaching and learning is bold. It's in our basements, and bringing it to the ground level is essential. The timing of the book is excellent."*

Carol Ann Tomlinson
Professor, University of Virginia
Author, *The Parallel Curriculum*

"A clear and insightful look at why teaching must be conceived as constant learning about learning. A genuine breakthrough in thinking, cutting to the chase about what the 'system' has to be to ensure learning of individuals en masse."

Grant Wiggins
Educational Consultant
Author, *Understanding by Design*

Breakthrough

Breakthrough

MICHAEL FULLAN
PETER HILL
CARMEL CRÉVOLA
Foreword by Richard F. Elmore

A JOINT PUBLICATION

CORWIN
PRESS

ns
dc

ONTARIO
PRINCIPALS'
COUNCIL
Exemplary Leadership
in Public Education

For information:

Corwin Press
A Sage Publications Company
2455 Teller Road
Thousand Oaks, California 91320
www.corwinpress.com

Sage Publications Ltd.
1 Oliver's Yard
55 City Road
London EC1Y 1SP
United Kingdom

Sage Publications India Pvt. Ltd.
B-42, Panchsheel Enclave
Post Box 4109
New Delhi 110 017 India

Printed in the United States of America.

Library of Congress Cataloging-in-Publication Data

Fullan, Michael.
Breakthrough / Michael Fullan, Peter Hill, Carmel Crévola.
        p. cm.
Includes bibliographical references and index.
ISBN 978-1-4129-2641-6 (cloth) — ISBN 978-1-4129-2642-3 (pbk.)
    1. School improvement programs—United States.
2. Educational change—United States. I. Hill, Peter. II. Crévola, Carmel.
III. Title.
LB2822.82.F85 2006
371.2'03—dc22

                                              2006001786

This book is printed on acid-free paper.

07   08   09   10   9   8   7   6   5   4

Acquisitions Editor:	Robert D. Clouse
Editorial Assistant:	Jingle Vea
Production Editor:	Jenn Reese
Copy Editor:	Jackie Tasch
Typesetter:	C&M Digitals (P) Ltd.
Proofreader:	Caryne Brown
Indexer:	Jeanne R. Busemeyer
Cover Designer:	Michael Dubowe

Contents

Foreword   **xi**
Richard F. Elmore

Preface   **xv**

Acknowledgments   **xix**

About the Authors   **xxi**

1. The New Mission for School Systems   **1**
   A System Stalled   2
   The Prescription Trap   8

2. Breakthrough Components   **13**
   The Triple P Core Components   15
      Personalization   16
      Precision   17
      Professional Learning   21

3. Transforming Classroom Instruction   **27**
   The Current Model   29
   The Crux of the Problem   31
   A Basis in Learning Theory   33
   The Breakthrough   35
      Key Assumptions   36
      The Four New Ingredients   36

4. Creating Expert Instructional Systems   **39**
   A Focus on Improvement by Design   40
   Expert Instructional Systems   45
   Assessment for Learning   47
   Lessons From Health Care   49
      Reforming Health Care   50

    Critical Care Paths   52
    Critical Learning Instructional Paths (CLIPs)   54

5. Building a Critical Learning Instructional Path   **57**
    Mapping the Instructional Path   58
    Measuring and Monitoring Learning   63
    Using the Data to Drive Instruction   69
    Classroom Organization   76
    Loops and Detours in the Critical
        Learning Instructional Path   78
    Beyond Early Literacy   79
    Locking In Ongoing Improvement   80
    Building the System   82

6. Breakthrough Leadership: A Way Forward   **85**
    What Is Needed   85
    Using Change Knowledge   87
    The Breakthrough Framework   89
    Breakthrough Leadership   95
        School Leadership   95
        District Leadership   96
        State Leadership and Other Big Players   98
    Conclusion   100

References   **101**

Index   **105**

Foreword

In my dictionary, *breakthrough* is defined as

> a sudden, dramatic and important discovery or development . . .
> [and/or] a significant . . . overcoming of a perceived obstacle,
> allowing the completion of a process.

The authors of this book describe a path, a process, a model that they think will take large educational systems from their current state of effortful but only marginally successful improvements to a completely different state, a high-functioning and powerful transformation unlike anything we have previously experienced. More than once, they use the term *tipping point* to describe this transformation. In social dynamics, tipping points are preceded by increased or pent-up capacity and demand, which seems incremental as it develops but builds to a point where it changes discontinuously to a completely different state.

My own work for the past 30 years or so has been shaped by the mantra, "steady work." This phrase comes from an ancient Jewish folk tale, captured by the essayist Irving Howe (1969; see also Elmore & McLaughlin, 1988) in which a villager is given the assignment of sitting outside the village gate to warn his fellow citizens of the arrival of the Messiah. After many decades, one of the villagers asks him why he continues to do this job. He replies, "The pay is meager, but the work is steady." My work has led me to an increasing appreciation of the power and resilience of the default culture of public schools—the deeply rooted beliefs, structures, artifacts, and symbols of an increasingly dysfunctional and obsolete set of institutions. Breakthroughs and tipping points are not the most appropriate metaphors in this world. Something like a large, thick rubber band might be more apt. The default culture stretches, seemingly to a breaking (tipping) point, and then it snaps back to where it was. The best ideas of reformers have, as yet, proven no match for the inertia of a powerful resident culture. I am increasingly convinced that the work of reform is not about "changing" the institutions and practices of schools but about deliberately displacing one culture with another—work not unlike moving graveyards. More deliberate and steady than discontinuous.

The advent of accountability has significantly juiced up the rhetoric of school reform. Easily available data on student performance have provided the fuel that reformers need to generate, at least rhetorically, a white-hot sense of urgency around school improvement. Those of us who work with schools on a regular basis—including the authors of this book—have unprecedented access to information about schools and their students to use it to bring this sense of urgency into the world of practice. In addition, the presence of systemic data has allowed us to identify exceptional schools, ones that seem to defy the default culture, and to use those exceptions to frame a vision of how schools might work in dramatically different ways. A sense of urgency, combined with some existence proofs, can convince one that *all* schools can do what a few schools have done. But, of course, a deep-seated feature of the default culture is that it has always allowed exceptional schools to exist, often in much larger proportions than at present, and these schools have never exercised a systemic influence (Elmore, 2004). In fact, one of the primary ways public education has legitimized itself is to point to these exceptions as evidence of the roiling activity of reform that will one day transform the entire system.

So *Breakthrough* is a deliberately contrarian book. It stakes out a view of school improvement that is at odds with much previous research and that paints a more optimistic view of the prospects for large-scale improvement than most earlier works. In this sense, it is an antidote to the work of others, mine included, that take a more skeptical view. Readers of this book, however, should be aware that they are entering a century-long debate over the conditions of success and failure in public schools, and they are preparing themselves to work on a century-old, deeply rooted set of cultural norms, practices, structures, and institutions. Whether you accept the authors' premise of discontinuous breakthroughs and tipping points or your working theory more closely resembles steady work, the forces that will determine your success will be the same. Know them well.

The authors give us a bold model, a model that captures the main elements of what advanced researchers and practitioners of school improvement have learned from studying exemplary schools over the past decade or so. The model joins the imperative of attention to the individual learning of students and educators to the conditions of the environment in which their work occurs. It connects a working theory of instructional practice with a working theory of the institutional conditions that will support that practice and the leadership skills and knowledge that will sustain it. There are several powerful ideas at the center of this model, among them the idea that instructional practice can meet a standard of precision without undermining its power or flexibility, the idea that learning must at the same time be personalized and generalized, the idea that formative assessment can be used to plot an improvement path at the individual and collective levels, and the idea that systems must reflect and respond in a timely way to the actual instructional decisions that teachers make. The authors are also careful to demonstrate that the overall design of their model is predicated on practices that are already in use, in a less systemic way, in many places. In fact, their argument that a breakthrough is imminent stems from the belief that several streams of practice are converging on a common target of opportunity created by the pressure of accountability for student performance.

Practitioners will, no doubt, find this book both a powerful guide to the work of school improvement and, perhaps more important, a source of constructive puzzlement. The authors make excellent use of research on primary school literacy practice to illustrate how robust theories of learning at the individual level can be generalized to the group, organization, and system levels. Literacy, however, is one subject among many, primary grade practices are much better developed than practices at other levels, and the problems of student learning and instructional practice, not to mention the development of teachers' knowledge and skill, vary substantially by content area and grade level. What this suggests is that, in addition to being a guide to practice, this book is also an invitation to practitioners to participate in a longer-term conversation—an extension and expansion of the book's general principles into other content areas, other age and grade levels, and other institutional settings. No doubt the authors' own ideas and practices will be informed over the longer term, as they have in the past, by their engagement in this conversation. The authors are, in this sense, courageous for bringing these ideas forward for use, debate, criticism, and revision. This book will be both a guide and provocation for future work on the critical questions of school improvement.

—Richard F. Elmore
Harvard University

Preface

Billions of dollars have been spent on education reform in the past decade and a half with results in literacy and math, at best, inching forward. This is not value for money, nor is it satisfying work for teachers, principals, students, and parents.

The thinking that brought us partial, small-scale success is not the kind of thinking that will make a substantial difference in the next phase of reform. Our primary purpose in writing this book is to present a radically different way of thinking about classroom instruction. Along with many others, we believe that the current model is in need of change—change that will transform practice in the same way that health care has been transformed over the past decade.

The groundwork for the new thinking has already been laid. This gives us optimism to think that, over the next few years, a breakthrough will occur in which the education community as a whole focuses on improving classroom instruction and adopts processes for turning it into a more precise, validated, data-driven expert activity that can respond to the learning needs of individual students. Improving classroom instruction on a universal scale is "the Breakthrough" we are seeking in this book. With a concerted effort from where education stands now, it is conceivable that a new "tipping point" (Gladwell, 2000) could be reached within five years.

In this book, we set out ideas for how such transformation can be accomplished. We show that it is essential to move away from what has always been done toward a new reality in which diagnostic practitioners, who have a solid core of beliefs and understandings, develop highly personalized programs that match the needs of individual students. The essence of our proposal is that education needs a system that will support the day-to-day transformation of instruction for all students—a system that is both practical and powerful.

Such a system must include all levels—the classroom, the school, the district, and the state. To transform instruction on a wide scale is to transform the entire system.

The key to this transformation lies in the smart use of data to drive instruction. Currently, many school systems collect data and feed it back to districts and schools. Much of this feedback is rudimentary and surface level. Where deeper feedback occurs, teachers are not helped to know what to do with it. Even if the data are better analyzed, teachers do not know how to translate the information into powerful, focused instruction that responds to individual students' needs.

Individualization, or what is now called personalization, has always been the bane of the busy classroom. So many students, so little time. Breakthrough is about making personalization feasible on a very large scale. We contend that this can be done without breaking the backs of teachers or breaking the bank of the public purse. Indeed, what is exciting about Breakthrough is that it will make teachers' work more energizing and rewarding, and it will make increased financial investment in the education system a wise thing to do for societal development.

Although the vision will not be realized overnight—it depends on decisions and serious investments by governments, school systems, and the private sector—there is much districts, schools, and teachers can do now to improve instruction along the lines suggested in this book. The ideas can help practitioners to improve their classrooms immediately, as they pave the way for the "big players" to invest in the systems and tools that classroom teachers need to conduct focused instruction on a daily basis.

We are by no means the first to suggest that the key to the transformation of learning in schools lies in the smart use of data to drive instruction. However, many pioneers of the use of data-driven instructional approaches have resorted to prescriptive approaches to create solutions that are workable in the complex and messy world of the classroom. Our book is not about prescription; it is about precision—the kind of precision that is tailored to the individual needs of each and every child in the classroom. It takes a system to deliver personalized precision.

Breakthrough work recognizes that it is time to shift the paradigm—and to do so in a way that both is practical and yields high-value return relative to financial and energy-based investments.

It is an invitation that educational leaders dare not turn down because the public school system in most countries is in a precarious state. In such times when something must be done, there is a fine line between breakthrough and breakdown.

The examples in this book came primarily from our work in early literacy, but the instructional system we propose applies to other learning domains such as math, science, history, and so on. Subject matter may differ, but the basic principles of learning, or rather *improving* learning, remain the same.

In Chapter 1, we make the case for a new mission for schools commensurate with the needs of the 21st century. If "No Child [is to be] Left Behind" (NCLB) in the United States, and if "Every Child Matters" in England, then schools must move from slogan to reality. The new reality is 90 percent or more success measured, for example, by students who achieve proficiency in literacy and numeracy by the time they are eight years old. In other words, proficiency that greatly enhances their chances for success in school and beyond. Society is the beneficiary both in economic and social terms. Chapter 2 shows that all the ingredients for success exist in one place or another. The goal is to bring them together in one concerted effort that permeates the system. Chapters 3 through 5 provide the shape of success concerning the kind of classroom instruction that will be needed. The final chapter focuses on the leadership infrastructure that must surround classroom instruction if Breakthrough is to be successful.

The reason we believe that the field of education has a chance to reach a new breakthrough is that there are many great beginnings now under way. We thank, in particular, those colleagues in several countries with whom we are working, too numerous to mention here by name. It is a great and crucial journey, and we are thankful to be able to learn from such groundbreakers. Alas, there is some distance to go.

Acknowledgments

Corwin Press gratefully acknowledges the contributions of the following people:

David T. Conley
Professor
Director, Center for Educational Policy Research
University of Oregon
Eugene, OR

Brent Davies
Professor of International Leadership Development
Director, International Leadership Centre
University of Hull
United Kingdom

Richard DuFour
Educational Author and Consultant
Moneta, VA

Dean Fink
Educational Development Consultant
Ancaster, Ontario, Canada

David Hopkins
HSBC iNet Chair of International Leadership
Institute of Education
University of London

Kenneth Leithwood
Professor
OISE / University of Toronto
Toronto, Ontario, Canada

Mike Schmoker
Independent Speaker and Consultant
Flagstaff, AZ

Thomas J. Sergiovanni
Lillian Radford Professor of Education
Trinity University
San Antonio, TX

James P. Spillane
Director, Multidisciplinary Program in Education Sciences
Associate Professor, Educational Social Policy
Faculty Fellow, Institute for Policy Research
Northwestern University
Evanston, IL

Carol Ann Tomlinson
Professor
University of Virginia
Department of Education
Charlottesville, VA

Grant Wiggins
President
Authentic Education
Hopewell, NJ

About the Authors

Michael Fullan is Professor of Policy Studies at the Ontario Institute of Education, University of Toronto. He is recognized as an international authority on education reform. His ideas for managing change are used in many countries, and his books have been published in several languages. His latest books are *The Moral Imperative of School Leadership, Leadership & Sustainability, Learning Places* (with Clif St. Germain), and *Beyond Turnaround Leadership.* In April 2004, he was appointed Special Adviser on Education to the Premier and Minister of Education in Ontario. He is currently engaged in several systemwide reforms in Ontario, Australia, England, and the United States.

Peter Hill is Secretary General of the Hong Kong Examinations and Assessment Authority, where he is leading an ambitious program of reform and modernization of the Hong Kong examination system. He has held numerous senior positions in school administration and educational research in Australia and the United States, including head of the school system in the State of Victoria, Australia, and Professor of Leadership and Management in the Faculty of Education of The University of Melbourne. More recently, he was Director of Research and Development at the National Center on Education and the Economy in the United States. Over the past decade, he has directed and assisted in a number of large-scale, comprehensive school improvement projects. His research interests are in the fields of assessment, school effectiveness and improvement, and instructional leadership.

 **Carmel Crévola** is an independent international literacy consultant, author, and researcher who works extensively in Australia, Canada, the United Kingdom, and the United States. Her focus is on helping systems align their assessment processes, instructional practices, and instructional leadership. She has pioneered new approaches to data-driven literacy instruction and has led several large-scale school reform initiatives in both Australia and the United States. She has 22 years of K–9 classroom teaching experience and was a school principal in Victoria, Australia.

CHAPTER ONE

The New Mission for School Systems

As societies have confronted the challenges brought about by globalization and new technologies, especially information technologies, the critical importance of education has become obvious to all. Political leaders have taken an unprecedented interest in public education and in charting a new mission for school systems.

The old mission was about providing access for all to basic education and access for a relatively small elite to university education. It is easy to underestimate the achievements of education systems in developed countries in securing universal education for all to the age of 15 or 16 years and in creating university places for between 20 and 50 percent of the student population. This achievement stands as one of the great social advances of the last century.

The new mission takes over where the old one left off. It is to get *all* students to meet high standards of education and to provide them with a lifelong education that does not have the built-in obsolescence of so much old-style curriculum but that equips them to be lifelong learners.

The benefits of having a good education are widely recognized, and the personal benefits are still a great incentive to individuals to do well. What are now much clearer are the substantial economic and social costs associated with *failure* to learn and failure to achieve one's full potential.

The authors have been working on the question of what is needed for the next radical breakthrough in education and have made

considerable progress in defining and implementing the key
elements: Hill and Crévola in specifying the new Critical Learning
Instructional Paths that will be required, which have been built
working with actual classrooms and schools; and Fullan in transforming the tri-level system of school/community, district, and state.
The Breakthrough we are seeking involves the education community
as a whole establishing a system of expert data-driven instruction
that will result in daily continuous improvement for all students in
all classrooms.

A number of authors have noted the ceiling effect that so often
accompanies literacy- and numeracy-improvement initiatives. The
diagnosis has been accurate (current strategies and conditions are
not powerful enough to take us to the next stage or breakthrough),
but no one has provided a clear picture of what the new paradigm
would actually look like and how it would function. The latter is
precisely what we have sought to develop, and that picture is the
essence of this book.

We believe that the ingredients necessary for a breakthrough
exist in one form or another in those countries with which we have
worked most closely: Australia, Canada, the United Kingdom, and
the United States. What is required now is to understand why domi-
nant current strategies do not work and what would be entailed in
creating a new approach that incorporates the essential components
into one integrated system that has the power to bring about the
transformation.

A SYSTEM STALLED

Within the current paradigm, even with all the best decisions and
with considerable resources for education, only partial, nonsustain-
able gains are being made. England's ambitious literacy and numeracy initiative started in 1997 with a flourish, moving in a short four
years from about 62 percent of 11-year-olds achieving proficiency in
literacy and numeracy to some 73 to 75 percent by 2000; then, outcomes plateaued for four straight years (Earl, Fullan, Leithwood, &
Watson, 2003).

The new mission for schools is to achieve 90 to 95 percent success. This is what it will take for societies to thrive in the complex
world of the 21st century. And the goal is not just about literacy and

numeracy scores. It is about learning to learn, about becoming independent thinkers and learners. It is about problem solving, teamwork, knowledge of the world, adaptability, and comfort in a global system of technologies, conflict, and complexity. It is about the joy of learning and the pleasure and productivity of using one's learning in all facets of work and life pursuits.

Much can be learned, especially from those reform attempts that appear to do a lot of the right things and yet still fall short, revealing fundamental limitations of a paradigm that misses certain key ingredients. We plan to identify the most salient, high-yield strategies and focuses, ones that are currently underplayed yet can be feasibly undertaken once identified. But first, let's start with the current situation to find out what is failing and what is missing.

A revealing place to start is the recent study by the Cross City Campaign for Urban School Reform (2005), which contains case studies of reform in Chicago, Milwaukee, and Seattle. All three school systems had the attention of political leaders at all levels of the system, focused on many of the "right things," such as literacy and math; all of the systems used obvious choice strategies such as concentration on "assessment for learning" data, invested heavily in professional development, developed new leadership, and focused on systemwide change.

And they had money—Seattle had $35 million in external funds, Milwaukee had extra resources and flexibility, and Chicago had more money than it had ever seen. There was huge pressure, but success was not expected overnight. Decision makers and the public would have been content to see growing success over a five- or even ten-year period.

The upfront conclusion of the case study evaluators:

> The three districts we studied had decentralized resources and authority to the schools in different ways and had undergone significant organizational changes to facilitate their ambitious, instructional improvement plans. The unfortunate reality for the many principals and teachers we interviewed is that the districts were unable to change and improve practice on a large scale. (Cross City Campaign, 2005, p. 4)

One of our goals in this book is to help the reader look beneath current reform initiatives to identify missing high-yield components.

Reform strategies are getting better (this is why we think, with additional concerted effort, education could soon reach a new tipping point), so it is crucial to zero in on the key problem areas. For us, the core problem is a failure to establish classroom routines and practices that represent personalized, ongoing, "data-driven focused instruction," which we will explain in subsequent chapters.

In the meantime, the issues in the Chicago, Milwaukee, and Seattle reforms help identify the missing ingredient, even though they appear to get most components right. Chicago, for example, appeared to have an impressive strategy:

Academic standards and instructional frameworks, assessment and accountability systems, and professional development for standards-based instruction are among the tools of systemic reform that are used to change classroom instruction. (Cross City Campaign, 2005, p. 23)

Here is a "standards-based" systemwide reform that sounds as if it should work. So what is the problem? In our view, the strategy lacks a focus on what needs to change in instructional practice. In Chicago, teachers did focus on standards and coverage, but in interviews, they "did not articulate any deep changes in teaching practice that may have been under way" (Cross City Campaign, 2005, p. 23). Furthermore,

Instructional goals were more often articulated in terms of student outcomes or achievement levels than in terms of instructional quality, that is, *what the schools do* to help students achieve. (p. 29, italics in original)

When systems tighten the focus on instructional goals, they get initial results (in the Chicago sample, schools had shown improvement on standardized tests over the past five years). This is the old mission of schools: to move from some 50 percent of the students achieving proficiency to 70 percent, but this is not good enough. The new mission is 90 percent and above, and gains need to be both sustained and deepened as portals for students to become independent learners.

The new mission will require substantial changes in daily instructional practice on the part of all teachers and parallel changes in the infrastructure to support such changes. In later chapters, we will identify the nature of these changes in classroom routines and in the infrastructure needed to support such transformation.

Milwaukee reveals similar problems in achieving instructional improvements while using greater decentralization in the context of system support and competitive choice. The focus was on literacy; a literacy coach was housed in every school in the district; considerable professional development and technical support services were available. Education plans for each school were to focus on literacy standards through (1) data analysis and assessment, and (2) subject-area achievement targets, including literacy across the curriculum.

Sounds like a convincing strategy. However, what is missing again is the black box of instructional practice in the classroom. The case writers observe:

> We placed the Education Plan in the indirect category due to its non-specificity regarding regular or desired instructional content and practices. (Cross City Campaign, 2005, p. 49)

More generally, the report concludes that while these serious districtwide reform initiatives "appeared" to prioritize instruction, they did so indirectly (through standards, assessment, leadership responsibilities). However, in the experience of principals and teachers, the net effect was that "policies and signals were non-specific regarding intended effects on classroom teaching and learning" (p. 65).

Our third case, Seattle, is a variation on the same theme. The game plan looks good. Standards defined the direction while the district's Transformational Academic Achievement Planning Process "was designed as a vehicle for helping schools develop their own strategy for (1) helping all students meet standards, and (2) eliminating the achievement gap between white students and students of color" (p. 66). As in Milwaukee, the district reorganized to support site-based management, including the allocation of considerable resources to schools. The case writers observe:

> The recent effort to become a standards-based district was one of the first sustained instructional efforts with direct attention to teaching and learning. However, the conversations district leaders had about standards *were rarely connected to changes in instruction.* (Cross City Campaign, 2005, p. 69, our italics)

The report continues:

> At the school level, finding teachers who understood the implications of standards for their teaching was difficult. (p. 72)

Without a more careful understanding of the new mission of schools, one would be hard-pressed to understand why the reform plans of Chicago, Milwaukee, and Seattle will not succeed. They will move scores forward—to a point. They contain glimpses of what will be required, but they fail to touch deeply day-to-day classroom instruction, and to touch it in a way that will get results for all. And what is more elusive is that the designers of the strategy believe that they have made instruction the centerpiece of the strategy. There is nothing more difficult to address than the case where people think that they are doing something when in reality they are not. It is not a case of deceiving others but rather of unwittingly deceiving oneself. When you don't know what you don't know, it is difficult to see what needs to be done.

Richard Elmore (2004) has been a relentless critic of the failure of school reform to get at the instructional core of schooling. Reform strategies, he argues, are "often not explicitly connected to fundamental changes in the way knowledge is constructed, nor to the division of responsibility between teachers and student [or] the way students and teachers interact with each other around knowledge" (p. 10). The crux of the problem, says Elmore, is that failing schools fundamentally lack what he calls *internal accountability:* "That is, they lack agreement and coherence around expectations for student learning, *and they lack the means to influence instructional practice in classrooms in ways that result in student learning*" (p. 234, our italics). We have already seen that external performance-based accountability is largely silent on how to achieve change in classroom practice, a point reinforced by Elmore: "In fact there is no well-worked-out theory of how you get from performance-based accountability to improvements in teaching and learning" (pp. 220–221).

In our own work with schools, we have sought to influence instructional practice by challenging the beliefs and understandings of teachers and school administrators, particularly around the notion that all students can achieve high standards given sufficient time and support. In initial discussions with school staffs, this notion was rarely rejected, but it was frequently qualified by all sorts of "Yes, but . . ." excuses as to why such a notion was generally true but didn't apply to some or even all of *their* students.

Elmore (2004) identifies another of the flaws in old mission work, namely, expecting linear gains to continue in student learning. The old mission demands steady movement upward; the new mission understands plateaus as stepping stones for going deeper. In referring to two schools with which he had close relationship, Elmore observes:

> Thornton and Clemente [schools] had initial gains, but their performance has gone flat and sits below target. This is actually a predictable pattern through the entire improvement process if you understand what it takes to move instructional practice at scale in schools and school systems. Significant gains in schools . . . are usually followed by periods of flat performance. These periods of flat performance are actually very important parts of the improvement process—they are the periods in which individual teachers consolidate and deepen the knowledge and practices they acquired in earlier stages, in which schools diagnose and identify barriers to the next stage of improvement, and in which they diagnose the next set of problems and look for the capacity to work on them. In existing accountability systems, these flat periods are seen as failures to improve, they carry heavy penalties. From the inside, these flat periods are actually important phases of improvement; improvement continues, even though performance is [temporarily] flat. (p. 248)

When performance plateaus or appears flat despite considerable effort to improve, one must look deeper in two respects: (1) to see if all the specific ingredients for improvement are actually being worked on, and (2) to realize that the next breakthrough may take additional time for new capacities to "kick in." Our work in York Region (just north of Toronto, Canada) illustrates some of these characteristics: a strong model, the need for greater precision in implementation, and an appreciation of the powerful platform that has been established for going to the next step of improvement (see Sharratt & Fullan, in press; see also Fullan, 2006).

External accountability systems are fundamentally flawed with respect to the plateau phenomenon. These schemes do not influence classroom practice effectively because they do not take into account the need to develop internal accountability in the school and the district. Thus, this kind of accountability cannot distinguish an improving school going through a flat period from a stagnant school that will never improve if left on its own.

If the school does not have its internal act together, it simply does not have the capacity to improve. In fact, it does not know *how* to improve, and no amount of external browbeating will produce capacity where it doesn't exist. As Elmore (2004) puts it:

> It seems unlikely . . . that schools operating in a default mode—where all questions of accountability related to student learning are essentially questions of individual teacher responsibility, will be capable of responding to strong, obtrusive external accountability systems in ways that lead to systematic deliberate improvement of instructional practice and therefore, the overall performance of its students implies a capacity for collective deliberation and action that schools in our sample did not exhibit. Where virtually all decisions about accountability are decisions [made by default] by individual teachers, based on their individual conceptions of what they and their students can do, it seems unlikely that these decisions will somehow aggregate into overall improvement for the school. (p. 197)

Elmore (2004) has nailed the problem, but his solution is outlined only in broad strokes: focus on increasing internal accountability and alter the incentive systems and working conditions so that schools can develop into "highly interactive, relatively coherent, informal and formal systems" of continuous improvements (p. 193). Elmore has many more helpful suggestions, but they tend mainly to point us in the right direction rather than provide ideas about *how* to proceed. We need to go from broad strokes to specific action without falling into the trap of prescription. This is the difference between our solutions of "data-driven focused instruction" and solutions bearing the mark of direct instruction. It is the difference between precision and prescription.

The Prescription Trap

If external performance standards do not get inside classroom practice, and if schools left to their own devices produce widely varied and inconsistent results, what is the solution? It is understandable that those desiring reform have moved toward greater prescription of what should happen in the classroom, especially if they justify their actions on the basis of moral purpose and evidence. Our own position is that prescription is a partial "old mission" solution that can obtain useful start-up results but is ultimately on the wrong track.

Our colleague Andy Hargreaves (2003) rejects prescription as downright dangerous: having cult-like qualities, being applied only to districts serving poorer communities, and creating a kind of apartheid of improvement, with better-off communities being able to pursue richer and deeper learning goals while poor communities become mired in drabness. Hargreaves contrasts prescription (which he calls Performance Training Sects) with collaborative communities (Professional Learning Communities). The former is characterized by knowledge transfer, imposed requirements, false certainty, intensive training, sects of performance, and the like, whereas the latter transforms knowledge, shares inquiry, engages in continuous learning, and builds communities of practice.

We think that Hargreaves's analysis is too crude and doesn't take us very far. It puts advocates of prescription on the defensive without giving them any convincing reasons to question their approaches, and it gives license to professional learning communities without any detailed strategy for accomplishing change in classrooms on a large scale. In later work, Hargreaves and Fink (2006) offer a more promising set of ideas for sustainable reform, but they don't deal with instructional transformation.

The solution must entail greater specificity without suffering the downside of prescription. But first, we must provide a more insightful appreciation of the strengths and limitations of prescription.

Prescription is appealing because it applies specificity to instruction with the promise of and in some cases the evidence of increased student performance. We will conclude that prescription has certain fatal flaws and that as a result, it will not get us to the deep changes required for the 21st century.

Prescriptive teaching often goes under the name of "direct instruction" and is used to refer generally to direct approaches to curriculum and instruction. In their meta-analysis of Comprehensive School Reform (CSR) designs, Borman, Hewes, Overman, and Brown (2003) indicated that, of the three models for which extensive research showed evidence of effectiveness for student achievement, two made extensive use of direct instruction approaches.

John Hattie's (1999) meta-analysis also indicates strong support for such approaches. He lists a large number of interventions and reports their mean effect size. The top three on his list are:

Feedback	0.81
Direct instruction	0.81
Prior achievement	0.80

So what is it about direct instruction or more prescriptive approaches that make them work, and why do they share the top spot along with feedback?

It comes as no surprise that feedback is among the top three interventions. It is, in fact, at the core of our Breakthrough solution. Good formative assessment can generate feedback for teachers to guide their teaching and feedback for students to guide their learning. The importance of prior achievement is also readily understandable. We argue later that knowing students' starting points is crucial because a student's readiness to learn is related to what he or she already knows and can do.

But what about direct instruction or prescription? Direct instruction is about the teacher being in control and directing the learning, using highly scripted lessons developed through detailed analysis of the curriculum and what it would take to learn it.

In schools in which teachers are poorly prepared and in which students have little prior knowledge to build on, direct instruction imposes its own form of discipline. It is structured and breaks learning into tiny steps so that underperforming students start to make progress. It puts teachers in control, teachers who may have spent much of their careers on the verge of chaos and disorder. This is why direct instruction has established a stronghold in inner-city schools and in schools in which there is constant disruption. Not surprisingly, most of the research into direct instruction has been conducted in these contexts. You rarely find such stringent approaches in affluent suburban schools, and really competent teachers simply reject direct instruction as de-skilling and overly prescriptive.

In situations characterized by a long history of failure, direct instruction often has success in getting students started in their learning, but the initial momentum and success are not sustained. There are a variety of reasons for this, including indirect ones such as superficial "adoption" decisions in which district and state advocates lose interest or are replaced by new leaders with different agendas (Datnow & Stringfield, 2000). But for us a more direct core reason for lack of sustainability is that while direct instructional approaches improve student achievement, students do not become independent learners, and when confronted with the new, they don't know what to do.

At the same time, it has to be acknowledged that more open approaches to learning in which the teacher acts primarily as facilitator have been even less successful. There is much to admire about direct instruction programs such as Success for All, which have accepted the chaotic environments of many inner-city schools and have tried to develop virtually teacher-proof materials and highly structured routines for classrooms to bring about a sense of order and purpose and to take away the hard work of planning the details of the teaching program.

Success for All and some other direct instruction programs have achieved remarkable short-term gains. Fielding, Kerr, and Rosier (2004) describe how Kennewick School District in the state of Washington, using rigorous direct instruction (mostly the Open Court program), moved Grade 3 reading results upward in the 13 elementary schools in the district. Between 1996 and 2004, the district average for third-grade proficiency moved from 74 percent to 88 percent, with several schools moving from the high 70s to 90s.

But in the end, all programs that make use of direct instructional approaches are trapped within a logic that fails students. The very act of scripting lessons means that we are talking about predetermined starting points with groups of students proceeding in a lockstep fashion. Yes, the best prescriptive programs start where individual students are, but the very act of putting teachers in control means that the students must follow the teacher, rather than the teacher following the students. In the end, we want to put the students in control of their learning process.

Boredom is what eventually gets both the teachers and the students. This is why many programs that rely on direct instruction are often discontinued by schools after a few years. These programs do not believe in the power of teachers as learners or of students as thinkers and problem solvers. As such, they cannot achieve long-term breakthrough results.

Direct instructional approaches lead to short-term gains, but a price is paid in terms of narrow control for teachers and little control for students. *Breakthrough* is an argument for changing the current model of classroom instruction to solve the very problems that direct instruction necessarily creates and reinforces. Direct instruction creates a perverse dependency to achieve short-term results. Our Breakthrough solution—a system based on focused instruction— matches the short-term effects of direct instruction while building the conditions for longer-term effects that will be shown to be far more enduring than those of direct instruction.

In short, greater precision does not mean greater prescription. We don't have to choose between loose professionalism and external imposition.

We are left then with a rather discouraging picture: Despite scads of money, the use of the best expertise to design and put into place strategies most likely to succeed, and the political will to stay the course, no one has yet cracked the classroom code leading to better instruction for all. Attempts to crack the code by specifying routines of instructional prescription give schools a false sense of progress with pernicious side effects. We can do better, much better.

We see the need to combine moral purpose with feasible, powerful strategies that give schools confidence that they can accomplish educational goals never before achieved. Our basic beliefs are founded on the moral purpose of education, not just for students but for teachers as well. And there are certain nonnegotiable beliefs:

- All students can achieve high standards, given sufficient time and support.
- All teachers can teach to high standards, given the right conditions and assistance.
- High expectations and early intervention are essential.
- Teachers need to learn all the time, and they need to be able to articulate both what they do and why they do it. (Hill & Crévola, 1999)

The difference between 1999 and now is that we think it is possible to realize these beliefs in practice—on a large scale, for all. The new mission of schools aims high: education that is truly for all. No one has yet provided a feasible platform for such grand accomplishments. Such a mission is within our grasp. We need to put our energy in the right combination of places. Subsequent chapters take us on this new breakthrough journey.

CHAPTER TWO

Breakthrough Components

A breakthrough will be achieved when virtually all students are served well by the public education system. This can happen only when the pieces required for systemic success are creatively assembled in the service of reform that touches every classroom.

In Senge's (1990) system thinking terms, schools currently have a lot of the needed "inventions," but not enough derivative innovations. Senge states that an invention or a new idea "becomes an innovation" only when it can be replicated on a meaningful scale at practical costs" (pp. 5–6). He elaborates:

> When an idea moves from an invention to an innovation, diverse "component technologies" come together. Emerging from isolated developments in separate fields of research, these components gradually form an "ensemble" of technologies that are critical to each other's success . . . The Wright brothers proved [in 1903] that powered flight was possible, but the McDonnell Douglas DC-3, introduced in 1935, ushered in the era of commercial air travel. The DC-3 was the first plane that supported itself economically as well as aerodynamically. During those intervening thirty years . . . myriad experiments with commercial flight had failed. Like early experiments with learning organizations, the early plans were not reliable, and cost effective on an appropriate scale.
>
> The DC-3, for the first time, brought together five critical component technologies that formed a successful ensemble. They were: the variable pitch propeller, retractable landing gear, a type of lightweight molded body construction. . . . radical

13

air-cooled engine, and wing flaps. To succeed, the DC-3 needed all five, four were not enough. (Senge, 1990, p. 6)

Our question, of course, is what are the specific critical components for a Breakthrough school system to take off? Before proceeding to answer this question, there is one other powerful metaphor that should guide our efforts. Eric Abrahamson (2004) in *Change Without Pain* (actually change with less pain than usual) compares change strategies that are based on "creative destruction" with those that stem from "creative recombination."

Too often, Abrahamson (2004) says, we start from the assumption that existing systems have little or no value and should be put aside in favor of brand-new solutions. Abrahamson calls this "the creative destruction" strategy, which more specifically results in the *repetitive change* syndrome:

The symptoms? Initiative overload, change-related chaos, and widespread employee anxiety, cynicism, and burnout. The results? Not only do relentless tidal shifts of change create pain at almost every level of the company and make organizational change harder to manage, more costly to implement, and more likely to fail, but they also impinge on routine operations, and render firms inwardly focused on managing change rather than outwardly focused on the customers these changes should serve. (Abrahamson, 2004, pp. 2–3)

Examples of repetitive change syndrome in school systems are legion. Although there are some exceptions (and even the positive exceptions, as we have seen, have not yet affected instructional practice), the experiences of the majority of educators are closer to Elmore's (2004) observation: "Local reform initiatives are typically characterized by volatility—jumping nervously from one reform idea to the next over relatively short periods of time—and superficiality—choosing reforms that have little impact on instruction or learning and implementing them in shallow ways" (p. 2).

The neglected and more powerful alternative, argues Abrahamson (2004), is "creative recombination." Change with less pain involves knowing what already exists in the system that can be revised, as well as knowing how you can redeploy and recombine existing elements in the system into new configurations. This, says Abrahamson, "is creative recombination in action" (p. 23).

The answer, then, is closer to home than we think. We have known since the early writings of the father of the study of modern organizations, Peter Drucker, that the failure to exploit existing innovations is more widespread than the failure to innovate in the first place. According to Abrahamson (2004), we are better off to "start with what you have lying around in the corporate [system] basement" (p. 26).

Education reform is at a stage where many of the components of successful large-scale reform are evident in schools' collective basements. One half of the solution is to seek out and identify the critical elements that need to be in place; the other half is combining them creatively. This is not simply a job of alignment, but rather one of establishing dynamic connectivity among the core elements.

We start in this chapter by identifying the three critical components that need to be at the core of any Breakthrough system.

The Triple P Core Components

Figure 2.1 displays the three core elements that form our Breakthrough system: personalization, precision, and professional learning. In this chapter, we establish their nature and importance, and in subsequent chapters, we provide more operational detail.

Figure 2.1   The Triple P Core Components

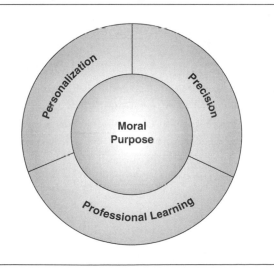

Recall Senge's (1990) criteria for innovation to flourish: All three components, not any two, will be required; the costs must be practical; and the benefits must be experienced on a wide scale—in other words, Breakthrough criteria. We must also reinforce our previous warning: Any overemphasis on one or two components at the expense of others will be divisive and dysfunctional. The glue that binds these three components is moral purpose: education for all that raises the bar as it closes the gap. For this to happen, the three Ps must be synergistically interconnected. When they are, the job becomes easier because each component leverages the others upward.

Personalization

Personalization, or what used to be called individualization, is the least advanced in practice of the three core components, although if anything it has a longer history than the other two. In recent years, there has been a renewed interest in personalization, thanks to educators such as Carol Ann Tomlinson (1998), whose work on differentiating classroom instruction has long been a staple resource for teachers and schools striving to implement a more individually tailored instructional program. Breakthrough strives to build on such good work with a meshing of the many components into a streamlined system of operations and processes.

Personalization is education that "puts the learner at the center" (Leadbeater, 2002, p. 1), or more accurately puts each and every child at the center and provides an education that is tailored to the students' learning and motivational needs at any given moment. Schools couldn't do this even when only 50 percent of the population of school-age children was being served, so how will they do it with virtually all children? Yet this is the Breakthrough standard we are setting.

Again, it has to be practical—less rather than more work for teachers. There are two aspects to personalization: namely, motivation to learn and pedagogical experiences that hit the mark particular for the individual. These aspects are obviously related. Students do not become engaged in learning unless the experience matches or inspires their needs, and exciting learning experiences generate further motivation. It is now well documented that, as children go from grade to grade in the educational system, their *engagement* with school and learning declines. This is a function of failure to personalize learning (and is related to inadequate linkages to the other two Ps—precision and professional learning).

Imagine a health care worker facing 30 citizens and having the responsibility for helping them establish healthy lifestyles. The health care leader has excellent standards at her disposal. It is clear where everyone should be heading. But the citizens are differentially motivated and are at very different starting points. Would inspirational teaching and clear standards carry the day? It would for a few, but not for many. The leader would have to have a way of diagnosing each individual's starting point to sort out where and equally how to proceed initially and every day thereafter. Heifetz and Linsky's (2002) observation about complex adaptive challenges is apt here: "The person with the problem is the problem, and is the solution" (p. 13). This is a personalization statement. Personalization is about individuals, but it is *relational*—between the teacher, the student, the home, and the school.

The mission of the school system is to make personalization a reality. But it must be universal—for all—or it will fail. Personalization is as much a collective as an individual phenomenon.

Aside from the immense practical problem of how to do it, there are dangers if personalization is carried out in the absence of the other components or without the moral purpose of serving all students to a high standard. Personalization often includes choice—by students and by parents. If the capacity to make choices is uneven, greater inequality will occur. Programs involving school choice within public systems, let alone systems that provide public funds to choose private educational options, are divisive and would not meet our Breakthrough criteria.

Instead, our view is that every public school and every teacher (individually and collectively) should be skilled at personalizing learning—putting the individual student (each one) at the center of learning. If this happens, the divisive tendencies to choose alternative schools will dissipate or otherwise operate within acceptable bounds of a system that is good for all. So the first challenge for the new mission of schools is how to make personalization of learning for everyone a practical reality. In the absence of pervasive personalization, the opposite will happen—mass production, a one-size-fits-all mentality that serves only those who benefit from the status quo.

Precision

To be precise is to get something right; to prescribe is to lay down rigid rules. Precision is in the service of personalization because it means to be uniquely accurate, that is, precise to the learning needs of the individual. Here a great deal of progress has been made recently in education's corporate basement under the practice of "assessment for learning" (using data as a tool for improving teaching and learning), there remains one fatal weakness—how to go from assessment to improvement of instructional practice in the classroom (again, for each and every child). Schools need to get assessment for learning out of the basement, clean it up, and creatively recombine it with personalization and continuous professional learning.

Remarkably, the theory of assessment for learning was laid out in clear and comprehensive terms many years ago by a number of writers. For example, 15 years ago, Sadler (1989) developed answers to two problems: (1) the lack of a theory of feedback and formative assessment in complex learning settings and (2) the puzzling observation that even when teachers provide students with valid and reliable judgments about the quality of their work, improvement does not necessarily follow (p. 119).

Sadler's (1989) main solution, way ahead of its time, was to focus on "how judgments about the quality of student responses (performances, pieces or works) can be used to shape and improve the student's competence by short-circuiting the randomness and inefficiency of trial and error learning" (p. 120). Consistent with our solution, Sadler said that *feedback* is the key element of formative assessment, but feedback qualifies as feedback *"only when it is used to alter the gap"* [of learning] (Sadler's italics, p. 121). Stated explicitly, Sadler observed:

> The learner has to (a) possess a concept of the *standard* (or goal, or reference level) being aimed for, (b) compare the *actual* (or current) *level of performance* with the standard, and (c) engage in appropriate *action* which leads to some closure of the gap. (p. 121, italics in original)

Sadler argued,

> Qualitative [personalized] judgments are invariably involved in appraising a student's performance. In such learnings, student development is multidimensional rather than sequential, and prerequisite learning cannot be conceptualized as neatly

packaged units of skills or knowledge. Growth takes place on many interrelated fronts at once and is continuous rather than lock-step. (p. 123) [as we shall see with our indicators in Chapter 5 of this volume]

For a system of continuous learning to work, standards must be communicated and be available to students. In a teaching setting, this presupposes that the teacher already possesses the knowledge of what is expected for given learners. However, "teachers' conceptions of quality are typically held largely in unarticulated form, inside their heads as tacit knowledge" (Sadler, 1989, p. 126). Such knowledge "keeps the concept of the standard relatively inaccessible to the learner, and tends to maintain the learner's dependence on the teacher for judgments about the quality of performance. How to draw the concept of excellence out of the heads of teachers, give it some external formulation, and make it available to the learner, is a non-trivial problem" (Sadler, 1989, p. 127). Not to mention the fact that some teachers' tacit knowledge may be vague or erroneous.

Feedback is at the heart of what is known as "assessment for learning"—a high-yield strategy of improvement that has come on the scene strongly in the past five years. The work of Black and Wiliam (1998a; 1998b) and Stiggins (2004), attests to the power and prominence of assessment for learning as a core precision-based component of reform.

As they do with most potentially high-yield solutions, systems have gone overboard on assessment as a solution. Systems have swamped schools with assessments and standards to the detriment of manageable and precise action. Too much of a good thing is a bad thing. Precision means refinement, not death by information overdose. Not only must feedback be relative to standards and performance but assessment for learning must also provide feedback to the teacher about *instruction* so that he or she can construct the instructional focus and set the goals of the lesson accordingly. Feedback, in other words, can be taken to extremes if it provides mounds of undigested information or if it is taken to imply impossible tasks for teachers, such as having to organize individual conferences with students every day. In Chapter 5, we spell out how feedback can be made more precise and immediately usable.

We see the glut of information in well-intentioned systemwide reform initiatives such as those reviewed in Chapter one in Chicago,

Milwaukee, and Seattle (Cross City Campaign, 2005). In those results-oriented districts, information on test scores was ubiquitous. The problem that we tackle in Breakthrough is not only how to make data more manageable but also precisely *how to link data to instruction on a daily basis*—something that so far has evaded even the most results-oriented districts. And we must do so without falling into the prescription trap of fostering student dependency. We must recognize that data-driven instruction is a strategy for improving pedagogy as a more precise causal link to student learning.

Breakthrough is intended to set the stage for classroom instruction in which the current sporadic data collection is streamlined, analysis is automated, and individualized instruction is delivered on a *daily* basis in *every* classroom. Now that is revolutionary.

Breakthrough represents a beginning for those who are nowhere near using data for improvement. For those who are down the track (and there are increasing numbers, thanks to the likes of Black & Wiliam, Stiggins, and developers of new approaches to using data, such as Good & Kaminski, 2002), Breakthrough is a call to take the next step in achieving greater precision in classroom instruction.

In our experience, even those who think they are well into assessment for learning soon realize that they have a way to go. Even in the best districts in this regard, the expertise lies in the hands of a few. The rhetoric of assessment for learning is abundant, but the knowledge in reality is very thin on the ground. The missing piece in most cases is a manageable system for going from data to instruction.

Breakthrough is about linking all the core pieces of the puzzle—within assessment for learning, in this case—and across the three core Ps of personalization, precision, and professional learning. Without our framework, educators often have many of the pieces, but they come from different puzzles. No wonder people cannot make a picture!

Educators have assessments, but they are often selected from bits of this and that, small pieces of the whole. Increasingly, teachers are helped in analyzing the data, receiving feedback in terms of scores and sometimes even skill analysis. The missing step and next piece is to make sense of the whole thing as *one unified picture* of where each student lies in terms of where to go next. For this, teachers need a manageable ongoing monitoring process that feeds into their knowledge for informing instruction.

Speaking of puzzle pieces, the systems we are talking about do not imply individual teachers would be doing these things, *but* collectivities of teachers. Elmore (2004), as we noted earlier, stresses that you cannot have effective external accountability in the absence of a capacity for internal (to the school) accountability. The most effective schools combine (1) individual responsibility and (2) collective expectations in a system that (3) aligns responsibility, expectation, and accountability, and that (4) incorporates external accountability demands (Elmore, 2004, p. 141).

Elmore (2004) found that:

> In these schools, collective expectations gelled into highly inter-active, relatively coherent, informal and formal systems, by which teachers and administrators held each other accountable for their actions vis-à-vis students. Teachers and administrators in this category of school were able to describe and interpret the formal external accountability systems in which their schools operated (such as testing systems, curriculum guidelines . . .) but in no case did those external systems seem to exercise the determining influence over their individual conceptions of responsibility, their collective expectations of each other or their students. (p. 193)

We are now approaching the third piece of our unified puzzle— the learning of teachers individually and as a group. Personalization requires precision, and precision demands ongoing learning.

Professional Learning

We have deliberately selected the term *professional learning* over the more narrow conceptual terms of *professional development* or *professional learning communities* because Breakthrough means focused, ongoing learning for each and every teacher.

You can't have personalization and precision without daily learning on the part of teachers, both individually and collectively. Over the past decade, education's hypothetical corporate basement (Abrahamson, 2004) has become cluttered with valuable bits and pieces of how teachers can best learn. It is time for some creative recombinations in the service of focused instruction.

In a detailed study of mathematics reform in California, Cohen and Hill (2001) argue that ongoing teacher learning is the key to linking new conceptions of instructional practice with assessment of student learning. They comment that the policy was intended to create coherence among elements of curriculum, assessment, and learning opportunities for teachers. But

> [s]uch coherence is quite rare in the blizzard of often divergent professional development that typically blows over U.S. public schools. Only a modest fraction of California elementary teachers—roughly 10 percent—had these experiences. Standards, assessments and accountability are more likely to succeed if they are accompanied by extended opportunities for professional learning that are grounded in practice. (Cohen & Hill, 2001, pp. 9–10)

Over the past decade, it has become a given that any major reform initiative must be accompanied by investments in professional development. Breakthrough is about how to refine and focus these investments in a way that will yield predictable continuous benefits for teachers and students.

The system is making progress, but not nearly enough as we saw from Cohen and Hill (2001; only 1 in 10 teachers evidenced significant learning, with no indication that the positive learning experiences would continue for the fortunate 10 percent). Confirmation of limited impact despite major focus and resources comes from Borman and Associates' (2005) investigation of mathematics and science reform in Chicago, El Paso, Memphis, and Miami.

Each city was the recipient of $15 million from the National Science Foundation's (NSF) Urban Systemic Initiative. Again, the strategy seemed to have all the right elements: a curriculum focus, a systemic orientation, plenty of investment in professional development, and an advanced conception of math and science learning. The policy and curriculum documents stated that "instruction should emphasize active learning and high order thinking skills while providing investigative and problem-solving opportunities for all students" (Borman and Associates, 2005, p. 4).

NSF's "Six Drivers Model" appears unassailable:

1. Implementation of a comprehensive, standards-based curriculum

2. Development of a coherent, consistent set of policies that support broad-based reform

3. Convergence of all resources that are designed to support the reform

4. Broad-based support from parents, policymakers, institutions of higher education, business and industry, foundations

5. Accumulation of a broad and deep array of evidence that the program does affect student achievement positively

6. Improving the achievement of all students, including those historically underserved

In reality, Borman and her colleagues (2005) found

> only tenuous links between professional development and classroom instruction for many teachers. Most teachers seemed to experience a disconnection between their professional development experiences and their day-to-day classroom experiences. (pp. 70–71)

Borman and colleagues also found that despite professional development sessions, which were based on extensive modeling of the new pedagogy focusing on specific instructional practices with students as active learners, little change in classrooms ensued. In their overall sample, they found through classroom observation that 78 percent of teaching remained teacher centered (didactic), 16 percent was subject centered, and less than 6 percent was student centered (p. 98).

Correspondingly, in evaluating classroom practices from the students' perspective (through observation and focused group interviews), Borman and colleagues (2005) found limited student engagement in learning:

> Based upon our results, if we consider the amount of class time during which students have opportunities to learn new concepts and acquire new skills, we are left with the unhappy reality that current professional development activities are not translating into the classroom with effective instructional strategies and content. (p. 153)

Recall that this limited impact occurred despite the fact that "both district and school administrators viewed the provision of professional development opportunities as a primary focus for reform implementation" (Borman & Associates, 2005, p. 216). Thus, educators appreciate that professional development is a *sine qua non* of success but have not converted this commitment into a high-yield strategy.

We can return to the larger Cross City Campaign (2005) evaluation of reforms in Chicago, Milwaukee, and Seattle to confirm that professional development is a central strategy but one that is problematic to implement effectively at the classroom and school levels.

Cross City Campaign (2005, p. 9) researchers found that most teachers experienced professional development as fragmented and not linked to their classroom practice, although districts were making some progress in improving the quality of individual sessions. In Seattle, for example, "professional development was a major tool for implementing reform"—one of the three key strategic standards (the other two are "Standards-Based Reform," and "Transformational Academic Planning Process"). As the researchers conclude, "the strength of the individual professional development offerings was sometimes quite high, but there was no overarching umbrella to integrate them. As one administrator observed, 'the ideas are good ideas and well intentioned. There's just no follow through'" (p. 80).

So, what's the solution? Generally, it involves turning the problem on its head. The solution does not involve attempting to coordinate centrally driven professional development, which (1) usually doesn't work or (2) can yield results only by resorting to behavioristic prescription, which we maintain is self-defeating.

Instead, schools need to work from the classroom outward—and glimpses of this solution are seen in the large-scale studies we just reviewed. Professional development works when it is "school-based and embedded in teachers' daily work" (Cross City Campaign, 2005, p. 10). And Cohen and Hill (2001) show that new policies and resources provide the potential for "new opportunities to learn, rooted either in improved student curriculum or in examples of students' work on assessments, or both" (p. 9).

The problem is that these grounded learning opportunities, even in situations with great system presence, are experienced by only a small minority of teachers (10 to 20 percent), and in all likelihood, these teachers are in the best circumstances. The kind of professional learning we are talking about in this book is available only for a minority of teachers and, even in those best-case scenarios, is not likely to be sustained for those teachers. This is why we are proposing a system change.

Let's be clear. We are not saying that only 10 to 20 percent of teachers are learning. Teachers learn every day. And most of them these days are learning to move literacy and math scores upward.

What we are saying is that the conditions for learning for the vast majority of teachers are not conducive to the Breakthrough we need to fulfill the new mission of schools.

How, then, do we make deeper daily learning a reality for teachers? Replacing the concept of professional development with professional learning is a good start; understanding that professional learning "in context" is the only learning that changes classroom instruction is a second step. Elmore (2004) got it right: "Improvement is more a function of *learning to do the right things* in the setting where you work" (p. 73).

We would have also italicized "in the setting where you work." Elmore (2004) elaborates on this fundamental insight:

> The problem [is that] there is almost no opportunity for teachers to engage in continuous and sustained learning about their practice in the setting in which they actually work, observing and being observed by their colleagues in their own classrooms and classrooms of other teachers in other schools confronting similar problems of practice. (p. 127)

It is not just a matter of teachers interacting; they must do so in relation to focused instruction. Professional learning communities, as we will see in Chapter 6, can contribute mightily to altering school conditions, but by themselves, they do not go deep enough into classroom practice, and they can even be (unwittingly) counterproductive if their interactions reinforce teaching practices that are ineffective (Cohen & Hill, 2001).

Our reluctant conclusion is that the most ambitious reforms have fallen miserably short of establishing the new mission of schools where virtually all students are engaged in their own significant learning. We need to start at the classroom, reconstructing the problem and the solution as one of embedding personalization, precision, and teacher learning into the daily experiences of students and educators. In so doing, we need to build an infrastructure that surrounds the classroom and will make such transformation inevitable. Moreover, it must be practically achievable.

Chapters 3 through 5 outline the instructional basis and nature of a practical solution to achieving education for all. It can be done only by transforming the last frontier of educational reform, classroom instruction, and this in turn requires a focus on using data to make instruction more precise. It will also require, as we take up in Chapter 6, Breakthrough leadership across the infrastructure.

There will be much more to be done beyond what we say in this book. Our goal is to make the case morally and intellectually clear and compelling. Despite failed reform efforts that have given us glimpses of a positive future—and perhaps arising from those efforts—we believe that we could be on the brink of a radical breakthrough. It is time to make learning an exciting and deeply rewarding enterprise for all.

CHAPTER THREE

Transforming Classroom Instruction

The next three chapters set out the core of the Breakthrough solution we envisage, which is something that has implications not just for classroom instruction but for all the layers that make up the school system as a whole.

Coherence between the multiple levels of schooling—the classroom, the school, and the larger system (e.g., district, state, and federal jurisdictions)—is an important precondition for successful school reform. The flow of schooling is disrupted when there is a lack of alignment and coherence. Teachers and school administrators receive mixed messages when no one direction is pursued consistently over time. Instead of flow, there is perpetual turbulence, and this tendency of systems to create turbulence confounds attempts to institutionalize systematic reform. When there is alignment, there is a much greater likelihood of sustained progress.

Our belief, however, is that system coherence is only a *precondition* for successful reform and that even when this precondition has been met, there are distinct limits to what can be achieved. For systems that have vigorously and successfully pursued school reform and have achieved a high degree of internal coherence, it is possible to quickly hit a ceiling and to struggle to show continued improvement. We have seen this in our own work in improving literacy outcomes in Australian elementary schools, and the same thing has been evident in England, where despite high internal coherence, improvement reached a plateau after a few years of marked growth.

For systems that have achieved internal coherence but are stuck and unable to move performance to higher levels, it is necessary to go deeper and address the most important condition for successful school reform, namely, the quality of classroom instruction. The new direction that we advocate is the complex and challenging task of transforming classroom instruction into a precision-based process that provides the teacher with the necessary information to make well-informed instructional decisions for all students on a day-to-day basis. Furthermore, we need to do this without falling into the prescription trap that we identified in Chapter 2.

Over the past 10 years, there have been major advances in thinking about the nature of classroom instruction and the interconnectedness of teaching and learning and equally major advances in thinking about ways of assisting teachers to be reflective practitioners. Much has been written about these advances, which to this point in time typically exist in a fragile state of implementation in a relatively small but growing number of instances of successful school reform. We say *fragile* because we are unaware of any instances in which it could be confidently claimed that the advances have become truly institutionalized and built into the very fabric of systems. We have been involved in several highly successful instances in which systems initiated and implemented school reform, but we are all too aware of the enormous task still to be achieved in extending and embedding this reform work and ensuring that best practice in classroom instruction becomes the norm and an institutionalized feature of schools and systems.

But this book is not about these changes, nor is it about the quest for answers to the problem of "scale-up" (extending change from a few sites to many). Rather, it is about where best-practice classroom instruction is taking us and what it is revealing about the limits of what can be achieved while working within the current paradigm. Our argument is that best practice itself is causing the questioning of the current model and its assumptions and is pointing to a Breakthrough in thinking and practice. Breakthrough involves changes with the power to make big differences and to transform the ordinary into the extraordinary.

What is more, we anticipate that the transformation will occur quite quickly and that there will soon be many examples in different locations of Breakthrough thinking about classroom instruction in action. Why do we believe the transformation will occur quickly?

We believe that many classrooms are already on the brink and ready to make the shift and that the conditions are right for rapid adoption. The "tipping point" will soon be reached, and in a matter of years, no school or school system will remain unaffected by this next phase of school reform, the phase in which the last frontier is reached and classroom instruction is transformed.

THE CURRENT MODEL

Why *instruction* and not teaching? Teaching is what teachers do, whereas what goes on in classrooms is very much an interaction between students, teachers, and resources in specific but constantly changing contexts in which the teacher is only one, albeit the most important, player. We therefore prefer the term *instruction,* which Cohen, Raudenbush, and Ball (2003) define as follows:

> Instruction consists of interactions among teachers and students around content, in environments . . . "Interaction" refers to no particular form of discourse but to teachers' and students' connected work, extending through days, weeks, and months. Instruction evolves as tasks develop and lead to others, as students' engagement and understanding waxes and wanes, and organization changes. Instruction is a stream, not an event, and it flows in and draws on environments—including other teachers and students, school leaders, parents, professionals, local districts, state agencies, and test and text publishers. (p. 122)

What this definition highlights is the enormously complex, interactive nature of instruction and the multilayered makeup of the influences that affect it. It also points to one of the great paradoxes in education. On the one hand, classroom instruction is one of the most widely experienced and public of activities, one that virtually every man, woman, and child can talk about from personal experience. After all, schools and schooling are ubiquitous, and teachers constitute one of the largest occupational groups in the workforce. On the other hand, classroom instruction remains a tangled web that has proven largely impenetrable to researchers. As a consequence, the knowledge base about classroom instruction is surprisingly tenuous, and in much policy discussion about school reform, the classroom remains something of a "black box."

In part, it is the highly interactive and unpredictable nature of the classroom that makes it such a tangled web. However much a teacher plans, however well-established the classroom rituals and routines, the unforeseen is virtually ensured. Under the current model, survival in the classroom depends on the seemingly intuitive capacity of teachers to draw on their experience to make lightning-speed micro-adaptations and on-the-run decisions in response to the unforeseen. Few other professions require the same degree of on-the-run decision making as teaching. Our Breakthrough solution rejects the notion that this should remain an ongoing expectation for teachers.

At one level, classroom instruction is totally transparent and carries no mystery, so much so that there is a common view that anyone can teach (as captured in the appalling saying: "Those who can, do, and those who can't, teach") and that it involves no deep technical knowledge or skill that cannot be quickly acquired by a reasonably intelligent and educated person. At another level, what constitutes powerful classroom instruction is ineffable and virtually impossible to define, let alone to systematically investigate and replicate.

However, there are other reasons why the classroom remains such a black box. As Burney (2004) comments, school education still operates on a model in which

> Individual teachers . . . work in isolation, forging their own methods of practice behind closed classroom doors . . . [T]eachers have come to regard autonomy and creativity—not rigorously shared knowledge—as the badge of professionalism. [This in turn has produced] highly personalized forms of instruction and huge variations in teacher quality and effectiveness. In effect, each teacher is left to invent his or her own knowledge base—unexamined, untested, idiosyncratic and potentially at odds with knowledge from which other teachers may be operating. (p. 528)

At the heart of the matter is the inescapable dilemma of classroom instruction: one teacher and (let's say) 30 students, all individual learners with different motivations to learn, different starting points, different strengths on which to build, and different areas of weakness that inhibit learning. Many strategies have been devised to respond to these individual differences, ranging from tracking or streaming to within-class grouping. However, each of these strategies is typically superimposed on an overall approach to instruction that ignores individual differences. Students are grouped into grades, based primarily on age rather than readiness to learn. Each grade has discrete curriculum objectives and performance standards, and each is taught over a single school year by the same teacher. At the end of each year, most students move to the next grade, to new curriculum objectives and standards, and to new teachers, regardless of how well they mastered the objectives of the preceding grade and with disregard for the relationships that have been built up between students and their teacher and for the knowledge that teachers have accumulated about their students.

The grade-progression model is a factory assembly-line model of schooling that assumes equal readiness to learn and equal rates of learning. The model persists despite overwhelming evidence that by around Grade 3, the achievement gap within a single grade may span five or more years of schooling. The model makes assessment of students to establish starting points irrelevant because the starting points are dictated by the curriculum, not by the readiness of students to learn. It denies individual differences. However, the differences remain and constitute the nub of the problem, the age-old problem of personalizing instruction.

It is this dilemma—wanting to respond to individual needs but having to do so in a class of 30 or so age-graded individuals without a clear idea how it can be done—that makes classroom instruction so problematic. In the absence of satisfactory answers, classroom instruction remains problematic, defying attempts to turn it into a precise, validated, data-driven, expert activity. Many teachers now find themselves looking for a way to break out of the endless cycle of change in which new ideas are adopted and soon abandoned as they in turn fail to solve the essential dilemma of classroom instruction. Finding the solution to the problem is the Breakthrough that is needed to move beyond the ceiling that successful systems and teachers find themselves hitting and to realize quantum improvements in student performance.

THE CRUX OF THE PROBLEM

Elsewhere, we have argued that meta-analyses and best-evidence syntheses of literally thousands of studies on effective teaching and classroom instruction point to the overriding importance of just three factors in explaining student achievement:

1. Motivation to learn and high expectations

2. Time on task and opportunity to learn

3. Focused teaching

The meaning and significance of the first two are well under-stood and require little comment. Students will not put in the neces-sary effort to learn unless they have the motivation to do so and unless there are consistent expectations from peers, parents, teachers, school administrators, and society at large that they will attain high standards. High expectations imply a belief in the capac-ity of all students to achieve high standards. They imply the exis-tence of challenging performance standards and ways of monitoring progress toward those standards. High expectations imply a belief that, with effort, all can achieve these standards. And they imply that everything will be done to get students to those standards.

Turning to the second factor, a massive amount of research evi-dence shows that effective learning requires adequate time spent directly engaged in learning. Learning takes time, and individuals need different amounts of time to learn the same things. These essen-tial truths are embedded in one of the earliest models of school learn-ing, namely that of Carroll (1989). An equally important corollary is that teaching requires good classroom organization and strong rou-tines for ensuring on-task behaviors that maximize engaged learning time and minimize disruptions and interruptions. We don't say this lightly because we know how much teachers struggle to establish classroom routines that enable them to teach effectively. Later on, when we illustrate our Breakthrough approach with reference to early literacy, we will emphasize how important it is that teachers are able to make use of such devices as task management boards, time clocks, book baskets, table organizers, and transition routines to ensure that students are able to operate productively when the teacher is engaged in small-group instruction.

The third factor, focused teaching, is harder to characterize. Scheerens and Bosker (1997) identify two separate factors, namely, a structured approach to teaching and types of adaptive instruction that can be managed by teachers. We believe that these characteris-tics are symptomatic of a single factor, namely, teaching that is focused on the learning needs of each student. We view focused teaching as:

1. knowing in a precise way the strengths and weaknesses of each student at the point of instruction through accurate formative assessment

2. knowing the appropriate instructional response and in particular when and how to use which instructional strategies and matched resources

3. having the classroom structures, routines, and tools to deliver differentiated instruction and focused teaching on a daily basis

Breakthrough involves finding satisfactory answers to the problem of matching the teaching and learning opportunities to the needs of individual students and providing expert, focused teaching in every lesson.

Two important points need to be made about focused teaching at this stage. The first is that the concept of focused teaching is consistent with widely validated views about the nature of learning. The second is that excellent examples of focused teaching exist, but rarely in regular classrooms.

A Basis in Learning Theory

Of the theoretical ideas that have been used to explain learning, probably none have been more powerful than Vygotsky's (1978) notion of the *zone of proximal development*, the critical zone where learning can be facilitated. There is no single zone for any individual; zones change from one domain to another and one minute to the next. Vygotsky also formulated a theory of *assisted development,* which is premised on the view that learning is maximized when a "more knowing other" (e.g., the teacher) is able to structure learning so that the difficulty of the task is in alignment with the individual needs of the learner. The teacher's role, to use Bruner's metaphor, is to scaffold the learning of the new task, revealing to the learner how to move from what he or she can currently do independently to a higher level of functioning (Wood, Bruner, & Ross, 1976).

The fundamental point is this: Instruction is powerful only when it is sufficiently precise and focused to build directly on what students already know and to take them to the next level. While a teacher does and must do many things, the most critical is designing and organizing instruction so that it is focused. Without focus, instruction is inefficient, and students spend too much time completing activities that are too easy and do not involve new learning or too little time on tasks that are too difficult and involve too much new learning or relearning.

Within one classroom, one might see, for example, Grade 3 students reading from the same pages of the set anthology. Some read the text easily and are presented with no challenges. For others, the text is at an appropriate instructional level, but the students are not provided relevant instruction to move forward. For yet others, the text is well beyond their instructional level, and they experience frustration, failure, and reinforcement of negative attitudes toward themselves and classroom learning. This is one-size-fits-all instruction. Within another classroom, one might see students reading different texts, having been matched to a text of an appropriate level of difficulty by the teacher on the basis of ongoing assessments of each student's text level and in the light of the particular objectives of the lesson. This is focused teaching. Needless to say, examples of both one-size-fits-all instruction and focused teaching can be found across all subjects and all grade levels.

When a learner makes connections and learning takes place, it is because of focused teaching. In an ideal world, the teacher would have precise and current knowledge of each student's starting points and also of what assistance each student requires to move to the next level. The way classroom instruction is currently conceived makes this virtually impossible. Most students nonetheless progress in their learning, even though their teachers are not fully conscious of the specific learning needs of each of the students they teach. Students stumble through on the basis of trial-and-error learning and more or less appropriate instruction. Teachers hold in their heads ballpark approximations of what has been covered and what needs to be taught at each grade level. Some teachers have a deeper knowledge in particular subject areas of the layers of development and their appropriate manifestation in terms of student understandings. But for the most part, the average classroom teacher begins each lesson with only a generalized knowledge of what students know and do not know and of where to focus instruction and provide assistance so that each student's learning needs are met. As a consequence, teaching in classrooms lacks the kind of focus and precision needed for all students to engage in powerful learning experiences. Students are left to fill in the gaps and find a way through the learning maze.

Teachers know this and are all too conscious of the gap between what they believe about learning and assisted development and the practicalities of making it happen in the busy classroom. Theory points to the importance of certain conditions being met for learning to occur, but within the current model, and given the realities of the classroom and the logistics of interacting with 30 or so students day in and day out, it is almost impossible for these conditions to be met for all students on a consistent and sustained basis.

Must this always be so? Is the notion of daily focused teaching for all students an unattainable ideal? We know that focused teaching is commonly observed in interactions between parents and children, for example, in fostering early language development through feedback and modeling. It is also commonly observed in situations such as sports coaching, private tutoring, or a range of other one-on-one contexts such as learning to play the piano. However, as numerous studies have confirmed, focused teaching is rarely observed in classroom settings (Tharp & Gallimore, 1988, p. 42). Focused teaching implies an intimate knowledge of each student and his or her capacities at any moment in time, along with classroom organizational settings in which this knowledge can be put to use. Such knowledge and such settings rarely exist currently. Breakthrough consists of finding ways to redesign classroom instruction so that focused teaching can consistently take place and so that instruction can indeed become a more precise, validated, data-driven, expert activity. The encouraging part is that it is possible to describe and give working examples of each of the tools and processes needed to make this a reality. The difficult part is making it happen on a large scale—every student, every teacher, every leader.

THE BREAKTHROUGH

It is our belief that focused teaching can and must be approximated within the regular classroom. We suspect that classroom instruction can never be designed so that it has the same degree of personalization and precision as can be achieved in, say, a one-on-one context, but we are confident that it can be made much more personalized and precise than it currently is.

For this to occur, however, classroom instruction has to be transformed. As we mentioned earlier, the needed changes are quite small and subtle, but their impact will be great. In the next two chapters, we will set out a strategy for bringing about the needed change and describe each of the changes in more detailed, concrete terms.

Key Assumptions

First, we make the assumption that two key ingredients of focused teaching already exist or can be established. These are:

1. A detailed map of a given segment of curriculum with clear specifications of the learning objectives, associated standards and targets, and indicators of student progress (For example, we might be talking about early literacy for students in Grades K through 2 or about algebra for middle-grade students.)

2. A detailed knowledge of how best to teach to these learning objectives in regular classroom settings, including explicit teaching strategies and methods and classroom routines and practices.

In other words, we make the assumption that we have the capacity to be explicit about what we are teaching for and that we know how to teach it.

We submit that there are many examples of good curriculum that provide the necessary degree of specification and of instructional programs that embody well-designed instructional approaches that work effectively in classroom settings when used at the right time with the right students. They are by no means universally observed in all classrooms, but there is no reason they should not be present.

The Four New Ingredients

Now, let's move to what is virtually nonexistent at the current time. There are four things on our list, all of them interrelated; none is sufficient of itself. They are:

1. A set of powerful and aligned assessment tools tied to the learning objectives of each lesson that give the teacher access to accurate and comprehensive information on the progress of each student on a daily basis and that can be administered without unduly interrupting normal classroom routines

2. A method of allowing the formative assessment data to be captured in a way that is not time consuming; to analyze the data automatically, and to convert it into information that is powerful enough to drive instructional decisions not sometime in the future, but tomorrow

3. A means of using the assessment information on each student to design and implement personalized instruction; assessment for learning being a strategy for improving instruction in precise ways

4. A built-in means of monitoring and managing learning, of testing what works, and of systematically improving the effectiveness of classroom instruction so that it more precisely responds to the learning needs of each student in the class

One can think of instances where current practice comes close to achieving one or more of the above, but we are aware of *none* that integrates all four. For example, DIBELS (Good & Kaminski, 2002) goes a long way to meeting the first three of the above in monitoring the assessment of early reading, although it is currently confined to the assessment of reading skills and misses out on the vital areas of oral language development, comprehension, and critical literacies.

If classroom instruction could be organized so that all four of the above were present simultaneously, this would lead to quantum ongoing improvements in the rate of student learning but, more important, to a transformational change in thinking about teaching. This is because, for the first time, classroom instruction would be organized so that teaching followed the student as opposed to the students following the teacher in pursuing common learning outcomes. Rather than beginning with instruction and ending with measuring student progress, instruction would begin with measuring what students know and are able to do; instruction would be designed on the basis of this information. In other words, the logic would be reversed. It would be a transformational change because, for the first time, systematic improvement would be a part of the very process of classroom instruction, making it an increasingly expert, validated (scientifically based) activity.

Currently, many instructional programs are designed with only the most general regard for students' starting points. In fact, some program developers say their programs are not only "teacher proof" but also "student proof." Lessons are scripted to enable them to be taught by any teacher (with proper training) to any student (of the same general level of schooling). Such programs often provide little or no internal capacity for personalization. What we are talking about is building personalization into the very fabric of classroom instruction. Borrowing Clay's (1993) words but applying them to the classroom context, we are talking about "a superbly sequenced program determined by the child's performance" (p. 9).

We believe that it is possible to achieve this degree of personalization and to design instructional programs that facilitate focused teaching on a daily basis within the regular classroom context. The following two chapters set out how this can happen. To break out of current modes of thinking about what is possible, we spend some time looking outside the field of education for an example of how similar paradigm change has occurred in another field that has confronted problems and challenges parallel to the personalization challenge of classroom instruction. The Breakthrough we are seeking requires us to move beyond the current confines of our thinking and gain inspiration from others who have embraced fundamental change. We must then create the new system by making it a practical and productive reality for all.

CHAPTER FOUR

Creating Expert Instructional Systems

The only way classroom instruction can become all the things we want it to be is through attention to *design* and the creation of expert instructional *systems*. The terms *design* and *system* sound cold and technocratic and run counter to a prevailing belief that teaching is irreducibly idiosyncratic—an "art" that is not susceptible to systematic and replicable knowledge (Elmore, 2004, p. 221). They are also terms that hit a raw nerve with those teachers who have had their professional competence challenged by external mandates and have had the stultifying and de-skilling experience of being required to implement instructional programs based on a one-size-fits-all approach.

The kind of instructional system we are talking about would place a premium on having highly trained and competent teachers who make the key instructional decisions in their classrooms. Precision does not imply prescription. On the contrary, we are talking about instructional systems that are constantly being developed and refined through teacher input and interaction. This is a hugely important point: Transformation of classroom instruction will only happen through meaningful engagement by the profession in the process.

For novice teachers and for the less competent, such systems would provide a guarantee of a high threshold standard of instruction for all students, whereas for the most experienced and competent, they would provide the opportunity to move to even higher levels of professionalism as coresearchers and codesigners of expert instructional systems.

A key question is whether teachers and administrators will find our proposal more work in an already harried day. The design we are proposing actually makes daily instruction easier, and above all, it motivates teachers both because it is simpler and because it directly motivates students. Students motivate even the most jaded teacher, especially students who are engaged in learning. Teachers are discouraged when they face scores of unmotivated children day after day. The vast majority of teachers want to serve the students if they can find a way to move forward. The Breakthrough will come when teachers *en masse* see that they can and are making a difference. There are many more nonblockers in the profession than blockers. If we can hook teachers on what is good for students, any remaining blockers will be stopped in their tracks. We stress this because we believe that there will be very few educators in this category since new Breakthrough understandings and processes will motivate scores of teachers who are now struggling, ambivalent, or even skeptical about whether they can make a difference. Moral purpose accompanied by a powerful pedagogy is unstoppable.

A Focus on Improvement by Design

It was Herbert Simon (1996) who first made the distinction between the sciences as being concerned with the study of natural phenomena and of how things *are* and the professions as being concerned with the study of the artificial and of how things *ought to be.* Simon saw architecture, business studies, education, engineering, law, and medicine as being centrally concerned with how things ought to be and with the process of *design.* For each of these professions, he held that the primary quest is finding the best way to achieve a particular goal. For the educator, the goal is to find the best way to promote learning.

Finding the best way is not a matter of daily discovery or serendipity but rather a matter of gradual improvement through attention to design and evaluation. Recall Senge's (1990) example of the DC-3. The same is true of many human systems. As we shall illustrate later on, health care has also improved dramatically through systematic attention to design and evaluation. The length of time in hospitals has decreased, patients are more informed and are in less discomfort and pain, health outcomes have been improved, and the costs of treatment have decreased (although total costs have risen because more people are participating). But health care has become more complex, doctors more specialist and expert, and nurses more highly educated and trained; hospital wards and standard treatment regimes are almost unrecognizable compared with those of just a few decades ago.

In school education, there is less evidence of systematic attention to design leading to gradual improvement of its core technology, classroom instruction. As many have remarked, classrooms have changed very little over the decades, and apart from some injection of new technologies that still leave most classrooms technologically more primitive than the homes from which students come, teaching looks much the same from one generation to the next. The teachers who taught us in the 1950s and early 1960s, were they still alive, would recognize all the essential features of a 21st-century English language or mathematics classroom and could in fact take over many lessons without much difficulty. There would be somewhat different norms and expectations with respect to student behavior and, of course, some new content and a different context, but in terms of core technology, instruction has changed very little. The same cannot be said of nursing. Our 1950s nurse would have difficulty recognizing almost any aspect of current procedures and would not be able to take over from our modern-day nurse.

Is this being too hard on teachers and on the teaching profession? True, we can all think of classrooms in which teaching has been transformed and can't be compared with what existed in the past. This has always been so. There have always been the innovators and the pioneers, although when examined closely, so many innovations are a rediscovery of what a previous generation of progressive teachers thought they had invented. We talk a lot nowadays about constructivism, about creating student-focused classrooms, as though these were cutting-edge ideas when in fact progressive educators have been exploring these ideas for almost a hundred years. There is little memory of the exciting reforms that were going on during the time of John Dewey, although some of us have vivid memories of groundbreaking but short-lived curriculum innovations of the 1960s, such as Man: A Course of Study (MACOS). Along with many other commentators, our conclusion is that on the margins, there is constant reinvention of classroom teaching, but the heartland remains unreformed.

This is not to say that teachers do not experience change. Just the reverse: Change is constant. Elmore (2004) echoes a number of writers in commenting that schools have learned to change massively in their surface structures while changing little at their core. Wave after wave of reform initiatives constantly disrupt the surface life of schools but rarely penetrate deeply into the classroom to bring about systematic improvements in instruction.

This is because in school education, there is no built-in mechanism that leads to ongoing improvement in classroom instruction. Wilson and Daviss (1994) refer to this mechanism, so well established in other fields, as the *redesign process,* which they describe as

> the integration of research, development, dissemination, and refinement by which innovations and the procedures that create them are originated, improved, and made affordable.

> . . . an institutionalized method of strategic, systematic change that works unceasingly to enact a vision of excellence as well as to redefine excellence itself when changing conditions make it necessary. (p. 22)

In China, teachers have light teaching loads in order to have time for lesson preparation and out-of-class contacts with students. Good teachers are recognized with titles and salary bonuses after they have been observed and have given demonstration lessons in front of large numbers of their peers (Cortazzi & Jin Lixian, 2001). In Japan, extensive use is made of lesson study, a form of professional development in which teachers come together to work on and improve a single lesson over many months, after which that lesson is made publicly available to all teachers (Stigler & Heibert, 1999). Many English-speaking countries over the last few years have introduced the concept of the classroom coach, who works with professional learning teams of teachers to improve classroom practice in a defined area of the curriculum (e.g., early literacy). These are all institutionalized approaches to improving the quality of classroom instruction, but none of these possesses the rigor or power to bring about sustained and systematic improvement in classroom instruction of the kind we envisage. They are on too small a scale, too limited in their scope, underconceptualized, too fragmented, under-resourced, and without a rigorous research foundation.

The educational research enterprise must bear much of the responsibility for this state of affairs. Too much educational research has proceeded on the natural sciences model and has been preoccupied with the search for grand theory and with describing what *is*, rather than focusing on issues of design and focusing on what *ought to be*. As a result, educational research often has little real relevance to practitioners and leads to few practical advances. Burkhardt and Schoenfeld (2003) note, "The research-based development of tools and processes for use by practitioners, common in other applied fields, is largely missing in education" (p. 3). They, along with other leading voices, including Sergiovanni (2000), have called for a shift in the whole educational research enterprise toward being a design science and art, making much more use of design experiments and adopting the metaphors of the design and engineering fields.

Interestingly, design-based research does not have to be atheoretical. Indeed, good design-based research may offer the best prospects for advancing certain kinds of theory.

> Importantly, design-based research goes beyond merely designing and testing particular interventions. Interventions embody specific claims about teaching and learning, and reflect a commitment to understanding the relationships among theory, designed artifacts, and practice. At the same time, research on specific interventions can contribute to theories of learning and teaching. (The Design-Based Research Collective, 2003, p. 6)

We see the kinds of instructional systems that are needed in the future as emanating from a design-focused conception of the role of research in shaping practice. In fact, we believe that instructional systems need to be conceptualized as ongoing research and development projects concerned with constant refinement and improvement. As we commented earlier, we also believe that the role of teachers needs to be correspondingly reconceptualized to enable appropriate levels of participation in and contribution to what would be a rigorously planned and conducted, large-scale, and adequately resourced research and development effort. Transformation of classroom instruction requires meaningful engagement of the teaching profession.

Along with Cohen, Raudenbush, and Ball (2003), we also believe that the focus must be on instructional *systems*, not just on one-off, disconnected programs, and that such systems require much more consistency in instruction than is currently common. Adopting a systems approach means looking at all the levels that contribute to improved student learning, whether at the level of the individual student, the home, the classroom, the school, the local district, the state, or the nation. It means systematically attending to all relevant factors at all levels in designing a coherent system of provision.

Something akin to a systems approach was taken by the school reform movement in the United States through the development of comprehensive school designs. This effort began with the nine designs promoted by the New American Schools Development Corporation (Stringfield, Ross, & Smith, 1996). Each design required many hundreds of hours of design work by teams of educators, all working to create a coherent and consistent approach to improvement, based wherever possible on best practices and findings from the research literature. Over a short space of time, a large number of designs were created and implemented in schools. Evidence regarding the effectiveness of 29 of the better known of these models is summarized in a meta-analysis of published studies by Borman, Hewes, Overman, and Brown (2003). The evidence is mixed and indicates that designs have varied substantially in their impact on student learning from those with no effect to those with substantial impact. Overall, the results achieved by school designs have been modest in relation to the effort expended on them.

Why have so many school designs failed to live up to initial expectations? There are several reasons:

- First, many designs have been underspecified. It is not just that they have focused on a relatively small part of the operations of a school; even in those areas on which they have focused attention, the detail and the necessary tools and support have often been missing.
- Second, design providers, at least initially, overestimated the capacity of most schools to bring about change and didn't think through their change strategies. The main complaint from the providers was that schools didn't implement their designs; from the schools' perspectives, they were being asked to change too much too quickly. The problem was compounded by the fact that most school designs were

implemented in the very schools with the least capacity for change, namely, struggling or failing schools.

- Third, many designs focused primarily on the supporting conditions for facilitating classroom teaching rather than on classroom teaching itself. When they did focus on instruction, it was more by way of general structures, overall philosophy and approach, and general advice and guidance. For example, they may have specified the learning time for a particular subject, the typical structure of lessons, and the classroom routines that teachers should adopt to facilitate teaching, but they may not have specified how to teach a particular segment of the curriculum. Those that did focus on the instructional core—and these tended to be the more effective designs—generally went for prescription rather than precision. They went for scripted lessons and a one-size-fits-all approach and so promoted teaching that had been expertly designed but lacked focus and precision.

- Fourth, such school designs relied on external programs rather than external instructional systems. Our idea is to put the teacher and student in the learner driver's seat, supported by a surrounding system that requires and enables focused instruction.

- Fifth, comprehensive school designs, ironically, are not *system* solutions. Despite the comprehensive requirement, the designs did not tackle the question of how to transform other layers of the system. And had they done so, they would have gotten it wrong—because their starting points were flawed (given that some models were vague and other models too prescriptive). Again, focused instruction as we outline in this book is the necessary starting point.

Because of the mixed results achieved by comprehensive school models, there is a danger that the concept of designs will be abandoned altogether. This would be a mistake. We need instead to go back to the drawing board and design expert instructional systems that will permeate every classroom.

EXPERT INSTRUCTIONAL SYSTEMS

So far, we have argued for a new paradigm of classroom instruction that delivers focused teaching using well-designed instructional systems in which the emphasis is on precision rather than prescription. At this point, we need to focus on another key aspect of Breakthrough, namely the need for an emphasis on creating *expert* instructional systems.

Expert systems have emerged out of work in artificial intelligence and have found application in a wide range of fields, including business, engineering, law, and the military. There has been considerable interest among educators in contrasting the thinking of novices to that of experts. There are also a few examples of attempts to apply this knowledge to building expert systems in the field of education and training, but these have typically focused on very narrow domains and have not been widely used in school classroom settings.

Expert systems seek to provide expert quality advice, diagnoses, and recommendations in real-world practical contexts. For example, to turn to the field of medicine, a general practitioner (the kind of doctor we visit when we have a health problem) may make use of an expert system in helping make a nonroutine, difficult diagnosis. The patient's symptoms are entered, and the system provides an expert opinion or suggests further tests to refine the diagnosis. It also finds all the relevant information regarding treatments. Expert systems are relevant in fields where the general practitioner needs access to instant expert advice in solving problems and making decisions.

Developing an expert system entails codifying the relevant knowledge of experts. This is no small task because experts are often not fully conscious of what they do. They find it difficult to express exactly what knowledge and rules they use to solve a problem and may forget to mention things that to them are obvious but that are not at all obvious to the novice. This means that first attempts to generate expert systems are rarely without flaws. Most expert systems begin as an initial prototype that is iteratively refined on the basis of feedback both from experts and from users of the systems.

We see classroom instruction as an activity that can be improved by making expert knowledge available to all teachers. It is manifestly evident that no one teacher can be an expert all of the time. Although most teachers are competent, few could be deemed to be expert in all areas of curriculum and instruction relevant to the classes they teach. The very nature of teaching and the relentless demands of the job leave little time and opportunity to develop deep expertise in the range and complexity of situations that a teacher will confront on a daily basis. Not every teacher is a master teacher, and no one teacher can, on the spot, consistently design the kind of lesson that a team of Japanese teachers, say, may have spent a year developing and refining.

Most important, we believe there is such a thing as expertise in teaching; that the nature of this expertise can be made explicit, so that it is capable of being replicated and validated; and that expert teaching translates into improved learning. Once again, it is important to reiterate that we are far from having to start from scratch. There is an extensive body of literature on effective teaching and powerful instructional strategies. The work of such experts as Marzano (2003) in the area of aligning the three levels of student, teacher, and school has done much to assist schools in recognizing that it takes more than a program to achieve success for all students. But still this has not gone far enough to get to the type of precision that we are proposing.

Expert systems involve a lot of work, which is why most that have been developed thus far deal with fairly narrow domains of activity. The kind of expert systems we envisage need to assist in defining what it means to perform expertly in a fairly broad domain of classroom instruction. However, we are fairly confident that in many relevant domains of teaching, good first approximations of the required expertise already exist. What is lacking are the systems to provide instant access to this expertise to classroom teachers at the point at which they need to make instructional decisions and a means of systematically validating and refining this knowledge base.

ASSESSMENT FOR LEARNING

At the heart of any expert system are two key subsystems. One is the knowledge base about what experts do in particular situations; the other is the case-specific data that relates to the situation at hand. Experts are nothing without data on current status: without it, all they can do is offer a highly qualified opinion. In an expert *instructional* system, the case-specific data consists of information on the previous and current status of learners. To use the language we are all familiar with, for case-specific data read *formative assessment* or *assessment for learning.*

Assessment for learning, as every teacher knows, is about obtaining feedback on the teaching and learning and using that feedback to further shape the instructional process and improve learning. Feedback to teachers enables them to focus their instruction; feedback to students enables them to monitor and improve their learning. The term *formative assessment* has been around for so long that it lacks power in conveying meaning and significance, which is perhaps why we are seeing alternative terms being used such as *assessment for learning* or *constructivist assessment* (Roos & Hamilton, 2005).

As commentators have pointed out for decades, assessment for learning has always been given inadequate attention and accorded a lower status than summative assessment. Most of the time, we see assessment *of* learning rather than assessment *for* learning. Rarely is assessment about information that will, on a day-to-day basis, guide and direct instructional decision making and improve learning.

These are not new thoughts. As we saw in Chapter 2, the case for making assessment for learning or formative assessment the centerpiece in the design of instructional systems was made by Royce Sadler (1989) many years ago. Paul Black and Dylan Wiliam (1998a, 1998b) have demonstrated that powerful evidence has existed for many years regarding the effectiveness of improved formative assessment as a means of raising standards. And Richard Stiggins (2004) and others have exposed the long history of mistaken beliefs that policymakers have entertained about the role of assessment in school improvement and have presented the case, once again, for a renewed focus on assessment *for* learning. We reiterate these thoughts but want to place them in the context of designing expert instructional systems. We also have a rather specific view of what is needed. To repeat what we said in the previous chapter, we need:

1. A set of powerful and aligned assessment tools tied to the learning objectives of each lesson, which give the teacher access to accurate and comprehensive information on the progress of each student on a daily basis and which can be administered without unduly interrupting normal classroom routines

2. A method of allowing the formative assessment data to be captured in a way that is not time consuming, to analyze the data automatically, and to convert it into information that is powerful enough to drive instructional decisions not sometime in the future, but tomorrow

3. A means of using the assessment information on each student to design and implement personalized instruction; assessment for learning being a strategy for improving instruction in precise ways

4. A built-in means of monitoring and managing learning, of testing what works, and of systematically improving the effectiveness of classroom instruction so that it more precisely responds to the learning needs of each student in the class

In the next chapter, we will outline what this might look like. Before doing so, however, we want to turn to another area of human-services provision that has gone through a transformation in thinking that parallels the changes we envisage for classroom instruction, namely, health care.

LESSONS FROM HEALTH CARE

Many teachers are doubtful whether their profession has much to learn about human services from other fields, particularly health. They rightly point out that education is not like health in that students are not sick or diseased. Education should not proceed on a deficit model but on a developmental model. We agree wholeheartedly with that view.

Some go one stage further and talk about the uniqueness of each student, arguing that in other areas of human service provision, personalization is not such a critical consideration. We agree about the need to acknowledge the uniqueness of each student, and in fact, our main motivation is to be able to respond better to individual differences rather than adopting one-size-fits-all approaches to classroom instruction. But we disagree that other fields do not also need to respond to individual differences. For example, in health care, every patient is an individual with a unique history and condition and must be responded to as such.

Finally, some go one stage further to say that teaching, unlike other forms of human service provision, cannot be improved through evidence-based, systematic approaches to improvement. They see teaching as a predominantly intuitive creative act and reject the rational scientific view. We believe that teaching should be very much art *and* science, and we see both perspectives combining naturally when education is viewed as being centrally concerned with the design of expert instructional systems.

Reforming Health Care

So what can we learn from health care? The essential message is that it has comparatively recently moved from being very like education to being much more an evidence-based design science. In our view, it is inevitable that education follow a similar path. Grover Whitehurst, the Director of the Institute of Educational Sciences within the U.S. Department of Education, expresses the underlying change in thinking as follows:

> Instead of thinking of the well-trained teacher, or primary-care physician, as an artist whose professional actions are creative expressions, the evidence-based perspective defines their roles as implementing and monitoring the success of research-validated protocols, and making adjustments as necessary to achieve the best outcome for the individuals under their care. (Whitehurst, 2004, p. 5)

We take it for granted these days that when our doctor prescribes a certain drug or recommends a particular procedure, it will have been evaluated in experimental trials to establish its effectiveness, and any side effects or risks will have been properly assessed and publicized. This indeed is what happens now because there are standards and enforcement of those standards. When something goes wrong with particular drugs, there are mechanisms for taking corrective action (although not soon enough in some instances). However, this has not always been standard practice. It is only in relatively recent times that medicine has had standards and that decisions have been made on the basis of scientific evidence rather than on the accumulated knowledge and experience of doctors.

Health care has benefited over the years from a number of macrolevel reforms that have improved outcomes for all. More recently, it has benefited from the adoption of new approaches that have transformed and made more personalized patient care in hospitals. There are important lessons for educators to be drawn from an understanding of these changes. We are aware that the health systems in some countries are still woefully inadequate in terms of wait times for crucial treatments and with respect to overall costs. Nonetheless, the new system designs currently being put in place in many jurisdictions are in the direction we are advocating.

Think of a hospital. In some ways, it is like a school. The wards are analogous to classrooms. Patients are grouped into wards depending on their general care needs. For example, there are maternity wards and coronary care wards, and so on. But each patient is an individual with a unique health history and conditions that need to be taken into account in treatment.

Fifteen years ago, if you went into hospital for a particular operation, there were few standard procedures or protocols for care. Different doctors within the same hospital and the same ward might specify quite different tests and treatments for essentially the same condition. They tended to give instructions to nurses rather than regard them as professionals in their own right with valuable insights into a patient's health and with a professional role to play in their treatment and care. In reality, there was wide variation in the quality of care. Hospitals were not patient focused, and the factory model was as much a feature of the hospital as it is today a feature of all too many schools. In addition, doctors worked in isolation and invented their own idiosyncratic knowledge bases and methods.

The impetus for change came from new models of funding. Faced with an uncontrollable spiraling of costs of hospitalization, it was necessary to provide incentives to cut out unnecessary and expensive tests and procedures, to reduce the length of patients' stay in hospitals while not compromising (and if possible improving) health outcomes. The new form of funding was called case mix funding. The government worked out the average cost of a standard operation and told hospitals that that was what they would get in future. If they were inefficient and patients spent longer than the average length of time in hospital, the hospital would lose money. If they decreased the time and costs of hospitalization, they would make a profit. Here was a real incentive to change.

Within a few years, there were significant savings as well as improvements in patient care. The change that delivered the saving was the application of what planners of projects had long referred to as critical path analysis. The methodology of critical path analysis was applied to health care and in turn became transformed into a methodology peculiarly suited to the health care context. These developments started in the United States but quickly spread to other countries and became standard practice in hospitals around the world. In short, a transformation in thinking occurred in health care.

Critical Care Paths

Several terms have been used to describe the new approach to health care, with the most common being *critical care paths;* other terms are *critical paths, integrated care pathways, clinical pathways,* and *care paths.* A critical care path in health care involves mapping the typical path for a given care process, such as a hip or knee replacement or a coronary bypass, including the timing and the sequence of actions and interventions necessary to achieve the desired outcomes. It seeks to anticipate at every stage the likely variations from the typical path and to specify what action to take when these variations occur.

Critical care paths help integrate the work of the many people who interact with the patient—the general practitioners, the specialists, nurses, radiologists, and so on. Unlike clinical guidelines or treatment protocols, critical care paths are data driven and dynamic. If evidence accumulates that time and cost parameters are exceeded consistently, causes are analyzed and improvements made to the care path.

The first step in developing a critical care path for a chosen group of patients is to construct a process map of the path taken by a patient from initial diagnosis to discharge. A multidisciplinary team will do this. Health care professionals will define the scope of the pathway and the desired outcomes. They will map the timing and sequence of steps and activities to be followed, identify who is responsible for each step and activity, and try to anticipate potential variations from this sequence. For example, in the case of a hip- or knee-replacement operation, it has been found that patients with diabetes present special circumstances that require detours to be built into the standard care path.

Critical care paths seek to be comprehensive and to take into account all aspects of the patient's care before, during, and after hospitalization. So they will specify the whole range of interventions, including clinical assessment, tests, treatment, medication, activities, patient and family education, and the discharge plan. For each patient, an expected length of stay is estimated, and the objectives of the hospitalization are stated up front. Critical care paths act as a single record of care indicating the extent to which the path was followed and if not, what variations occurred and why. Recording variations is vital because it is the variations that in the end lead to improvements or to detours or loops that accommodate specific patient needs and circumstances.

In the early 1990s, the second author became involved in a project to develop and implement critical care paths for a private hospital group in Victoria, Australia. At the time, the project generated a great deal of excitement; this was in the early, heady days of the reform movement. It was the first time that senior specialists had sat down with general practitioners and senior nurses to work on an integrated approach to patient care. The initial multidisciplinary team meetings were difficult and contained a lot of surprises for everyone. Specialists often did not know in detail what their colleagues did, and they were unaware of the depth of knowledge and the insights of the senior nurses. Some specialists had always ordered lots of tests, some requested fewer, but the number of tests seemed to bear little relationship to health outcomes. Over time, the meetings became easier, more open, and more productive, and care paths were developed for the main high volume/high cost procedures.

The next stage was developing a system for monitoring the implementation of the critical care path and collecting data. A primitive computer program was developed that was later refined to look much more like a modern expert system. The nurses were given the responsibility of entering the data, so attention had to be given to developing easy ways of recording and entering the information. After the first three months, an initial database had been created, and the multidisciplinary team met to look at the data, which were displayed by means of tables and charts.

The meeting was electrifying. Nobody had seen this sort of data before, and it transformed the conversation. From this point onward, the data rather than the opinions of the noisiest and most senior individuals drove the conversation. Gaps and redundancies in the care path became obvious, and blockages were quickly identified. Patterns behind patients with poor health outcomes could be seen in the bar charts, leading to a refinement of the care path or to building in more detours and loops.

These days, critical care paths are no longer at the cutting edge of health care in hospitals. But their impact has been substantial (a recent Google search of the term *critical care paths* identified about 1,550,000 entries). They have led to systematic approaches that have brought dramatic improvements in outcomes. These improvements have been made through careful design and ongoing data-driven refinement of critical care paths, in which the effects of individual changes might be very small—too small to reliably detect without statistical analysis—but which cumulatively result in substantial impacts.

So, what are the lessons for education? As Cohen, Raudenbush, and Ball (2003) comment: "Education is not medicine, and few educational interventions come close to the precision of many in medicine" (p. 133). However, as they also note, if education was reconceived and if instruction was redesigned as a set of regimes or systems, the prospect exists of systematically comparing different regimes and systems and progressively improving teaching and learning.

We need, then, data-driven systems that focus on the learning needs of *all* individual students and teachers. And the solution must be replicable on a large scale at practical costs. The solution must be simultaneously efficient and effective.

CRITICAL LEARNING INSTRUCTIONAL PATHS (CLIPs)

For the past few years, we have been seeking to apply the above notions to the design of classroom instruction for early literacy. This has emerged out of two related projects. The first, the Children's Literacy Success Strategy (CLaSS), is a school-improvement project of the Catholic Education Office, Melbourne, and has been operating since 1998 in more than 300 Catholic elementary schools in Victoria, Australia. The second, Building Essential Literacy (BEL), is an initiative of Mondo Publishing in New York City and has been operating in schools across the United States since 1999.

In both projects, we have been challenged by teachers who find themselves at the cutting edge and want to move to a higher level. The search for greater precision and for a means of achieving focused teaching on a daily basis has prompted us to seek to develop easy-to-use formative assessment tools, to codify the pathways followed by students as they become literate, and to formulate "if this, then that" type expert advice about which teaching strategies to use, given certain patterns of student literacy behaviors.

Based on this work, we believe that the concepts of carefully designed expert systems and critical paths can, with appropriate adaptations, work in the same way that they have in transforming other fields such as health care. We have coined the umbrella term *critical learning instructional path* to refer to this approach within a school education context, although later on we will use the abbreviation CLIP as a shorthand way of referring to this concept.

Literacy teaching is highly time-sensitive. There is only a narrow window of time in which students must learn to read and write. Students who fail to become literate by the end of their second or third year of schooling rarely catch up with their peers. Literacy is extremely important, but it is only one part of the curriculum. The mandate of educators is very broad in scope, and we don't see this approach as immediately applicable to *all* outcomes in school education. CLIPs would focus, at least in the first instance, on *core* learning that is critical and time-sensitive.

We view CLIPs as devices for bringing expert knowledge to bear on the detailed daily decisions that every classroom teacher must make in teaching a coherent domain of the curriculum. Fortunately, we know a great deal about early literacy—more than enough to construct a typical learning pathway and to identify some of the more important variations typically encountered as students become literate. (The same applies to a lesser extent to some other domains of learning.) Furthermore, we can specify appropriate instructional strategies for a given profile of literacy behaviors. Although all this expert knowledge is available, it is not in the hands of teachers in their daily classroom setting. The rationale for developing CLIPs in areas such as early literacy would be to give schools and teachers access to validated knowledge and provide them with powerful tools to manage instruction in the most expert way possible. Chapter 5 provides examples of what this might look like in the context of teaching young children to become literate.

CHAPTER FIVE

Building a Critical Learning Instructional Path

To achieve a Breakthrough in thinking about classroom instruction, it is important to begin to generate concrete images of what the new thinking might look like in practice. This chapter seeks to do just that. Inevitably, in the early stages of seeking to change classroom practice, attempts to visualize the new will be crude, and in key aspects the necessary vision and foresight will be lacking. However, our aim here is to provide not a detailed blueprint but rather the broader picture. We anticipate that over the coming years, as teams work on actual blueprints, the concept of Critical Learning Instructional Paths (CLIPs) will have many different manifestations, and only time will tell which will be the most promising.

Talking in the abstract has its limitations; therefore, we want to contextualize our discussions with reference to a defined area of classroom instruction. We have, therefore, decided to illustrate what a CLIP might look like in practice with reference to *early literacy* for students ages 4.5 to 8 years (K–3). Literacy is a key area of the curriculum as it involves core learning that is critical and time-sensitive; also, it is the area of instruction that we, together with the educational research community generally, know most about. It is also an area in which, despite massive efforts in recent years, significant numbers of students continue to experience problems that dog them for the rest of their lives.

Later on, we will talk about the application of CLIPs to other areas of the curriculum and to other levels of schooling. But let's move one step at a time. We know that whenever attention is paid to one area of the curriculum, there is a hue and cry about the other areas. However, there are times when it is important to prioritize concerns. We hope that high school history teachers (to mention just one other group) will agree that if we could do a much better job in the early years in getting all students to high levels of literacy, their job would be so much easier. Of course, in the longer term, we hope that teachers will want to explore the implications of our approach for high school history and other curriculum areas. But right now, our focus is on early literacy.

We begin with the task of constructing a CLIP in our chosen domain. We then consider how teachers can measure and monitor student learning on a daily basis and how the assessment data can be turned into information that teachers can use to plan instruction and deliver focused, precision teaching. Next, we address the issue of those detours that may be necessary for special groups of students. This is followed by a brief discussion of the process of locking in ongoing improvement and of systematically validating and extending the knowledge base and the quality of the expert advice. Finally, we touch on issues involved in designing and testing a working instructional system that has these characteristics.

Mapping the Instructional Path

Educators are familiar with syllabuses, lists of objectives, scope and sequence charts, and grade-level standards as ways of expressing the outcomes to be achieved through the curriculum. How do traditional ways of mapping curriculum outcomes differ from how we would construct a CLIP? The short answer is not a great deal, but there are some key differences. We envisage that development would proceed with very similar, perhaps identical, notions of end points as embodied in the best currently available examples of content and performance standards.

Our CLIP must be able to guide and monitor learning and teaching on a day-to-day basis, and so it needs to be detailed. Without detail, we cannot achieve precision. Traditional curricula often focus on the end points of a *journey,* whereas an instructional path is about the route taken by the average learner in getting there, including the detours or loops followed by significant numbers of learners who, for one reason or another, can be expected to take alternative pathways at certain junctures.

The notion of a journey, but with different starting points for different individuals and with some individuals needing to take departures from the main pathway, is a helpful metaphor in thinking about CLIPs. With this metaphor in mind, consider the task of mapping the path followed by young children as they become literate. The first step is to start with a description of the terrain as a means of clarifying exactly what it is that students are doing when they embark on the journey of learning to read and write.

This is no trivial matter. In recent years, there has been a tendency to seek to reduce and confine literacy curricula to skills development and to ignore the wider cognitive demands of what it means to become literate, including (in addition to skills) the acquisition of knowledge (content), conceptual understanding, and supporting affective outcomes (e.g., a love of reading). Thus, we see drilling in various reading skills, such as phonemic awareness, and improvements in student ability to decode text, but, unsurprisingly, little evidence of improved fluency and comprehension. We are also concerned at the absence of any real attempt to evaluate the oral language development of students as it relates to literacy development generally and as it relates to reading comprehension in particular.

A similar situation has prevailed in mathematics, with many traditional textbooks overemphasizing skills at the expense of conceptual understanding and applications of mathematical understandings in real-life contexts. Fortunately, this tendency has been reversed in recent years, and mathematics curricula and textbooks have been produced that avoid a reductionist approach and place a much greater emphasis on conceptual understanding.

Any CLIP must begin with a comprehensive description of the overall terrain that brings out all the salient features of the journey to be taken by the learner. The next stage in the mapping process is to identify the key *stages* of the journey. Returning to our early literacy example, in working with schools, we have highlighted six developmental stages of reading that typify the paths taken by young learners. Although we present these stages as a developmental continuum, they do not necessarily form an invariant sequence. It is not uncommon to see students exhibiting a range of behaviors that span a number of stages, depending on the text that they are reading.

1. Pre-Emergent

   During this stage, students are not yet reading published texts. They can often read their own name and maybe one or two other sight words. Students in this stage have limited oral language knowledge and limited knowledge of how print works. This is often referred to as the role-play stage of development

2. Early Emergent

   These students are beginning to apply their knowledge about how print works. They are beginning to apply some early conventions and concepts about print as they read simple texts. They have a small bank of letter knowledge and high-frequency sight words. They can read some known texts relying heavily on memory and picture cues. Their ability to read fluently is limited as they rely heavily on one-to-one word matching and finger pointing.

3. Emergent

   During this stage, students can reconstruct familiar texts and can respond to and discuss texts. They are more consistent in matching the written word to the spoken word. Their letter/sound knowledge is developed to the point at which they are beginning to problem-solve on unknown words and to experiment with reading simple texts. Emergent students have a growing bank of high-frequency and sight words.

4. Beginning

   Beginning readers understand that a text represents a consistent way of telling a story or relating information. They have begun to use a variety of strategies to decode and comprehend text and are able to adapt their reading to suit different text types. Their letter/sound knowledge is now consolidated. Reading fluency is a major focus in this stage.

5. Transitional

   During this stage, students are beginning to integrate all cuing sources to make meaning from text. They have the ability to make connections between what they already know and what is new. They can relate to the text and make meaningful predictions and self-correct independently. Transitional readers read in a phrased and fluent manner, using intonation and language structures to support the construction of the message.

6. Established

Established readers have an understanding of the characters, events, situations, and relationships in narrative texts. They make personal connections with the characters, evaluate situations, and make judgments based on their experiences. Students in this stage read a variety of nonfiction material for research purposes and for pleasure. Established readers can and need to read for longer stretches of time; they can read silently and adjust their style of reading to reflect the text and the purpose. They can decode unknown words rapidly and fluently.

There is nothing new in the above. Many similar characterizations of the reading process exist. In practice, these stage descriptions would be further elaborated and illustrated to better characterize the way in which typical learners progress during their first three or four years of schooling.

Having broken the journey into stages, the next step is to identify medium-term objectives or outcomes statements and more detailed, short-term *indicators of progress.* The outcome statements provide medium-term goals for instruction—for example, what the typical student will have achieved by the end of the school year. Such statements are common in modern curricula and are typically expressed in terms of grade-level performance standards.

The indicators of progress are less commonly found in most curricula or programs. They enable the teacher to trace the steps made by the learner as he or she moves from being a novice to having partial understanding or mastery to acquiring competence. In CLIP, indicators provide the basis for monitoring the progress of each individual student within a given stage of development. They provide *feedback* to teachers on the effectiveness of their instruction and specific *instructional foci* for their daily lessons. They also form the basis for providing *feedback to students* to enable them to self-monitor their learning, to evaluate their performance, and to know what constitutes an improved performance.

In our experience, the development of a comprehensive set of indicators is one of the most vital steps in constructing a CLIP. What should these indicators look like? In some areas, they will resemble and have the tight specificity of behavioral objectives, and they will be amenable to temporal sequencing. This would apply, for example, to indicators of progress in acquiring letter-sound knowledge. In other areas, indicators will be of a kind that cannot be expressed as either present or not present, that require the use of meta-criteria in arriving at overall judgments of quality, and that are not hierarchical in the sense that one logically precedes or follows another. This characterization would apply, for example, to indicators of progress in comprehending interpretive meanings of texts.

The following is a small sample of indicators relevant to the fourth of the previously described six stages, namely the Beginning stage of reading.

- Uses picture clues when appropriate for confirming or assisting prediction
- Uses text structures such as repetitive language patterns, rhyme, and story structure to assist predictions
- Displays an understanding of narrative structure, that is, the beginning, middle, and end of a story
- Focuses on larger chunks of text rather than single words
- Understands the importance of visualization (mental images) to comprehend text
- Rereads to confirm meaning
- Skim reads when searching for clues to confirm predictions

Once again, these are abbreviated descriptions of indicators, each of which warrants further elaboration and illustration. Each needs to be accompanied with further details that specify more precisely the observed behavior and the level of performance that a Beginning stage reader might be expected to exhibit. The indicators do not have to be confined to cognitive behaviors and can include indicators for other domains.

Taken together, the overview of the terrain to be covered, the descriptions of the stages of the journey, the outcome statements, and the more detailed indicators for each stage provide a comprehensive map of the expected path to be followed by students as they learn to read. They would also be accompanied with exemplars, including video clips and samples of student work. Once again, we must stress that this is not new. Examples of these elements are present in existing curricula, so we are by no means starting from scratch, but much more needs to be in place. We need to establish dynamic connectivity among the core elements.

MEASURING AND MONITORING LEARNING

Having mapped the CLIP followed by students in the early years as they become literate, the next task is to design a system for measuring and monitoring their progress with reference to the key stages and the indicators. Focused teaching requires that teachers have precise and continuously updated information on students' starting points and on their progress along the way. Even in the best of currently available instructional programs, this condition is only partially satisfied.

The first step in measuring and monitoring learning is to specify the key outcomes that will be assessed throughout the CLIP. Next, a comprehensive schedule of pre- and posttesting must be established to measure the beginning and end points of students within each school year and with reference to the key stages of the journey as captured in the outcome statements for each stage. The result of this testing is an explicit profile for each student. Finally, attention must be given to the design of procedures for monitoring student progress *on a daily basis* with reference to the indicators. These all form part of the instructional regime of the classroom. Together, they constitute a set of nested cycles of activity as indicated in Figure 5.1.

At this point, it is important to reflect that although Figure 5.1 is unremarkable from a theoretical point of view, it is alien in terms of everyday practice. Conventionally, little or no time is devoted to pretesting to establish starting points and to building up a profile for each student. This is because instruction follows the curriculum rather than the learner. A systematic assessment process that includes initial preassessment or screening of all students in each classroom is the essential means of establishing the starting points for instruction.

Figure 5.1   Cycles of Assessment and Instruction

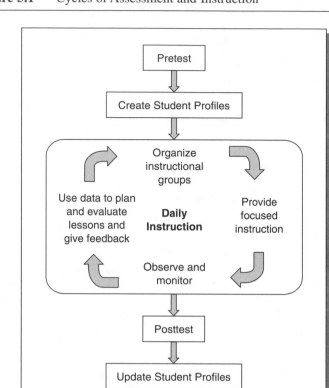

Too few classroom teachers take or are provided with the time to find out just what the student knows before launching into their preconceived and preorganized grade-level programs, which operate regardless of the students in the classroom. It is one thing to be a Grade 2 or Grade 6 teacher, and a whole other thing to be the teacher of this class of Grade 2 or Grade 6 students. For students to make significant learning gains, instruction must be focused on meeting the needs of the individuals within the classroom and not merely on following the set anthology, core reading program, or prescribed textbook.

Let us begin with the first of the developmental tasks, namely, that of specifying the key outcomes to be assessed systematically at the beginning and end of each school year. The aim is to obtain as complete a picture as possible of each student on *all* dimensions of significance. Figure 5.2 sets out an assessment regime for eight key

Figure 5.2   Example of a Reading Assessment Regime for Grades K–3

Outcomes	K	1	2	3
1. Oral Language Development	All	All	At Risk	At Risk
2. Benchmark Text Level/ Comprehension	All	All	All	All
3. Fluency	All	All	All	All
4. Concepts About Print	All	All	At Risk	At Risk
5. Phonemic Awareness	All	All	At Risk	At Risk
6. Letter Identification	All	All	At Risk	At Risk
7. Phonics	All	All	All	At Risk
8. Word Knowledge	All	All	At Risk	At Risk
9. Vocabulary	All	All	All	All

outcomes in learning to read across four years of K–3 schooling. (For the purposes of this illustration, we omit writing outcomes.)

It can be seen that this is a comprehensive assessment regime, but one in which some outcomes are assessed in the early years but not in the later years. For example, it is anticipated that there will be no need to assess early reading behaviors (e.g., letter-sound, print concepts, and phonemic awareness of all Grade 3 students, although it will be necessary to do so for at-risk students who continue to have difficulties in these areas.

As a plan for assessing students at the *end* of the year, the assessment regime represented by Figure 5.2 is not remarkable except for its comprehensiveness. Many schools collect such information and use it in preparing report cards on students. But few adopt an assessment regime that involves pretesting, and from experience, we know how difficult it is to persuade schools to do so. Even when teachers recognize the need for establishing students' starting points, they can think of many reasons why it is too hard a task. They include:

- insufficient time to obtain a detailed assessment of 25 to 30 students, especially when it involves one-on-one assessment
- not having access to appropriate assessment tools
- not knowing what to do with the data once it has been collected

These are all legitimate issues, but not reasons why it should not be done. An effective assessment regime needs to provide information on students' instructional needs as well as acting as a first alert for students who need direct intervention. Once these needs are established, teachers can more easily group students and provide focused teaching that is targeted at the appropriate level. Focused teaching means ensuring that students are operating in their zone of proximal development, where competence and challenge are aligned. The hallmark of the expert teacher is that he or she operates in a focused instructional mode consistently on a day-to-day basis for all students. At the end of the year, information gained by using the same assessment tools allows valid measurement of the gains made during the year.

The first requirement for making this doable is a set of quick, easy-to-administer assessment tools. In recent years, thanks to the increased attention that policymakers have paid to early reading, a wide range of assessment tools has been developed for use in schools, notably DIBELS (Good & Kaminski, 2002), and these can readily be administered by classroom teachers. Once again, however, we believe that what currently exists does not go far enough in terms of providing a comprehensive assessment of all the aspects of reading development. The following two examples are adapted from Crévola and Vineis (2004b).

Figure 5.3 shows a segment of an oral language assessment for use with K–3 students. The instrument provides a means of assessing some of the most complex structures of oral English that students can listen to and understand. Thus, it is a measure of receptive language. It consists of a series of sentences of increasing structural complexity. As students repeat the sentences, the teacher notes any substitutions, omissions, transpositions, or expansions of words and phrases that occur when the sentences become too difficult, similar to taking a record of reading. A score of one point is awarded for each sentence repeated correctly in every detail. Altogether, a student is presented with 15 sentences and five sentence types. The complete instrument can readily be administered to a student in about five minutes.

The second example is a record of reading used to determine a student's instructional text level and to provide measures of comprehension and oral reading fluency. Figure 5.4 shows a segment of the record for assessing students at Level E (as part of a continuum of text levels ranging from Levels A to R).[1] Having selected an unseen text[2] of what the teacher believes to be an appropriate level of

Figure 5.3   Segment of Oral Language Assessment

Set 2
Type

1	*That car in the yard used to be my Dad's.*	
2	*The boy on the horse is holding the reins.*	
3	*Over the holidays Mom bought me some sneakers.*	
4	*These are the pilots who fly the big planes.*	
5	*The girl made a snowman up on the mountain.*	
	Subtotal	

Figure 5.4   Segment of a Record of Reading

RECORD OF READING			
LEVEL: E		**Instructional**	**Easy**
Planting A Garden	**%**	**90%–94%**	**95%–100%**
Student _____ Teacher _____	**Errors:**	**18–11**	**9–0**
Date _____			

PG	Running Words: 182 Errors: [ ] Fluency Total: [ ]	Fluency #
2.	How do gardens grow?	4
	Gardens have to be planted.	9
3.	Some gardens look neat and some look messy.	17
4.	What do you have to do to plant a garden?	27
	All plants grow from seeds.	32
5.	So you need to get some seeds?	39
	Where can you get the plant seeds?	46
	You can get them from the store or	54
	you can get them from the plant!	61

difficulty for the student, the teacher tells the student the full title of the text, gives an overview of the text, and sets a context for the reading. The teacher then reads the title page to the student and asks the student to independently read the text aloud while the teacher takes a record of reading, noting the reading behaviors and errors made by the student. At the conclusion, the teacher uses the guide in the upper right corner to determine whether the student is reading at his or her instructional level (see Crévola & Vineis, 2004a, for further details)

Initially, this is a time-consuming assessment because if the teacher is not aware of the current reading level of the student, then it is a hit-and-miss affair until an accuracy level is determined. In subsequent assessments, the teacher will be much more precise in the selection of an appropriate level of text. This is not a new process for K–3 teachers of reading. Taking a record of reading for students using pieces of continuous text is now common practice across Australia, Canada, England, and the United States. Such tools need to be integrated into a unified set of assessments.

By noting the last word read after one minute and the number of errors made, the teacher can compute the total minus errors Words Per Minute (WPM) of the student and thereby generate a measure of oral reading fluency. Finally, through the use of questioning and a simple scoring rubric, the teacher is able to make an assessment of the student's ability to recall information and his or her level of comprehension of the text. The use of both fiction and nonfiction as part of the assessment process is essential to supporting the development of critical and analytical aspects of reading development. In this way, the one assessment activity is able to generate systematic information on student performance relevant to three of the reading outcomes identified in the assessment regime. It is critical to select assessment tools that are interrelated and provide a complete picture of the starting points for subsequent instruction.

The above examples seek to illustrate that the systematic pretesting of students at the beginning of each year need not be an unduly onerous task; it will certainly provide the teacher with a great deal of information on and insight into the strengths and weaknesses of each student. The data collected as a result of implementing the pre- and posttesting assessment regime is used to create student profiles, about which we will say more later. Right now, while we are focusing on ways of measuring and monitoring progress, we turn to considering procedures for the daily monitoring of student progress with reference to the indicators.

It will be recalled that the indicators are intended to enable both the planning and the monitoring of instruction on a daily basis. In other words, they are the key to the daily instructional cycle shown in the center of Figure 5.1. The teacher will typically select one or two indicators and make these the focus of a lesson. Invariably, the teacher will select certain indicators to form the focus of whole-class instruction and other indicators that will be relevant to different groups of students within the class. It is, however, in the small-group situation that the teacher is able to directly observe and record the performance and behaviors of individuals. Both the planning of the instruction and the monitoring of student progress are facilitated through the use of a Focus Sheet, an example of which, adapted from Crévola and Vineis (2004b), is shown in Figure 5.5.

As can be seen, for each student in each instructional group, the teacher indicates with a tick or a cross whether or not the student demonstrated understanding of the behavior represented by the indicator during the small-group session. The process is thus quick and manageable. It brings the planning of instruction, the recording of student progress, and the evaluation of teaching into a single, seamless process. Not every student is assessed in each session. The number assessed depends on the number of instructional groups in the class and how many rotations the teacher can achieve in a given session. However, over the course of a week, it can be expected that each student's progress will have been recorded at least twice and more frequently for struggling learners. While each daily assessment results in just a tick or a cross for each student on each indicator, because each indicator will be addressed in more than one lesson, the teacher is able to track those students who consistently exhibit the observed behavior and those who do not. In this way, the data necessary to drive instruction is at hand. Currently, teachers tend to keep lesson plans separate from student evaluations. The Focus Sheet is a device for integrating the two to provide ongoing data to guide instruction on a day-to-day basis. It replaces prepared lesson plans.

USING THE DATA TO DRIVE INSTRUCTION

Having addressed the issue of measuring and monitoring student progress, the next issue is that of *using* the data so that instruction is characterized by precision and teaching is focused on the learning needs of each student. There is no value in assessing students if it does not impact learning and instruction. Today, many teachers remain daunted by the amount of assessment data that they have available to them. Besides a method of capturing formative assessment data in a way that is not overwhelmingly time-consuming, they

Figure 5.5   Focus Sheet: Reading Grades K–3

FOCUS SHEET: READING K–3									
Class:			**Date:**						

Whole Class

Title:
Foci:
1.
2.
3.
Comments for future instruction:

Small Group

Group 1 **Instructional Strategy:** ❑ Oral Language ❑ Language Experience ❑ Read To ❑ Shared Reading ❑ Guided Reading ❑ Reciprocal Teaching	Materials: Title: Text Level:	Students							
Foci:	1.								
	2.								
Comments for Future Instruction:									

Group 2 **Instructional Strategy:** ❑ Oral Language ❑ Language Experience ❑ Read To ❑ Shared Reading ❑ Guided Reading ❑ Reciprocal Teaching	Materials: Title: Text Level:	Students							
Foci:	1.								
	2.								
Comments for Future Instruction:									

Whole Class

Share Focus:

Comments for Future Instruction:

Sample

need a method of analyzing the data automatically and converting it into information that is powerful enough to drive instructional decisions—not sometime in the future, but tomorrow. Leaving aside for the time being the automation of these processes, we now focus on *using* the data.

The first step is to generate summaries of students' starting points through the creation of *Student Learning Profiles.* These enable teachers to summarize all the assessment data generated through pretesting, to identify strengths and weaknesses, and to determine each student's stage of development. Once this is done, teachers can effectively group their students to tailor the instruction in both whole-class and small-group learning settings. An example of a Student Learning Profile is shown in Figure 5.6 (adapted from Crévola & Vineis, 2004b).

Figure 5.6.   Sample Student Learning Profile

Student: *Tanya*	Class: *1C*		Date: *Sept, 24*
Outcome	**Range**	**Score**	**Stage**
1. Oral Language*	0–15	12	*Beginning*
2. Benchmark Text Level/Comprehension*	A–Z	E	*Beginning*
3. Fluency*	0–110	30/E	*Emergent/Beginning*
4. Concepts About Print*	0–18	18	"
5. Phonemic Awareness*	0–52	42	"
6. Letter Identification	0–54	52	"
7. Phonics	0–60	36	*Emergent*
8. Word Knowledge*	0–20	16	*Beginning*
9. Vocabulary	100	20	*Emergent*

Reading Stage:

Pre-emergent ☐   Early-emergent ☐   Emergent ☐   Beginning ☒

Transitional ☐   Established ☐

Comments:

Tanya is strong in her concepts of oral English and is operating at a Beginning stage in reading accuracy and comprehension. She is weaker in her vocabulary and phonics knowledge. She will benefit from extra attention to phonics skills during the skills block and in classroom learning tasks. She will need to work on developing a larger bank of high frequency words in order to process more difficult texts with speed and accuracy.

*Keyed to instruments published in Crévola & Vineis (2004b)

What follows may at first appear complex, but our experience has shown that if teachers are carefully assisted through the process and given the time to ask questions and discuss their understandings, this process soon becomes second nature. It provides teachers with the type of information and direction that actually make the task of personalizing instruction less daunting.

As shown in Figure 5.6, Tanya has just commenced Grade 1. Her Benchmark Text Level score indicates that as a reader, she is at the Beginning stage. However, she lacks fluency when reading simple texts. There are indications that she is lagging behind in her vocabulary and phonics skills. The teacher will likely have other students at the same stage as Tanya, while others will be at a more advanced stage. In using the data about each student to drive instruction, the teacher will make use of an Instructional Strategies Matrix that ties together assessment scores, stages, and appropriate instructional strategies.

An example of such a matrix is shown in Figure 5.7.[3] The Instructional Strategies Matrix is the key to aligning curriculum intentions, assessment information, and classroom instructional strategies for all students in the classroom.

On balance, Tanya is a Beginning reader, although with the noted areas of weakness. In small-group teaching sessions, Tanya's teacher is likely to make most use of the teaching strategies of Oral Language, Language Experience, Read To, Shared Reading, and Guided Reading to assist Tanya in making progress. However, in planning lessons, the teacher will also need to include those indicators relevant to the Early Emergent stage that relate to Vocabulary and Phonics development, particularly letter-sound correspondence and blending sounds.

Being able to make a direct link between a student's results on a set of assessments, his or her stage of development, and specific teaching strategies relevant to that stage of development is an essential part of developing a CLIP. The process makes diagnosing students' strengths and weaknesses and planning instruction explicit, and as such amenable to ongoing improvement and refinement. Of course, using CLIPs also assumes that teachers have a common language and a common set of understandings about different teaching strategies. Until recently, this did not exist in many school systems. Now, most teachers in early grades can name the strategies they use, and while many may make use of only a few (particularly Guided Reading), there is a substantial professional literature providing

Figure 5.7.   Sample Instructional Strategies Matrix

Assessment \ Stage	Pre Emergent	Early Emergent	Emergent	Beginning	Transitional	Established
Oral Language*	0–4	5–7	8–12	13–15		
Benchmark Text Level*	Not on Text	A–B	B–D	D–G	G–K	K–S
Fluency*	N/A	20 WPM Level B text	30 WPM Level D Text	40 WPM Level G Text	40 WPM Level I Text	90/110 WPM Level M/N Text
Concepts About Print*	0–6	7–14	15–18			
Phonemic Awareness*	0–15	16–35	36–52			
Letter Identification	n–nn	nn–nn	nn–nn			
Phonics	n–nn	nn–nn	nn–nn	nn–nn	nn–nn	nn–nn
Word Knowledge*	0–5	6–10	11–15	16–20		
Vocabulary	n–nn	nn–nn	nn–nn	nn–nn	nn–nn	nn–nn
Small-Group Instructional Strategies	• Read To • Oral Language • Language Experience • Shared Reading	• Read To • Oral Language • Language Experience • Shared Reading • Guided Reading	• Oral Language • Language Experience • Shared Reading • Guided Reading	• Oral Language • Guided Reading	• Guided Reading	• Guided Reading • Reciprocal Teaching

← Grade K →

← Grade 1 →

← Grade 2 →

← Grade 3 →

*Keyed to instruments published in Crévola & Vineis (2004b)

coherent and detailed accounts of the half dozen or so main strategies relevant to teaching young children to read (Crévola & Hill, 2000; Crévola & Vineis, 2004a).

In training teachers to implement a CLIP, considerable attention needs to be given to developing teachers' understanding of and competence in using a range of powerful instructional strategies. Our experience in using the matrix shown in Figure 5.7 has been that teachers who have previously struggled to articulate what they know about their students experience a rapid growth in their articulation of students' achievements when using this matrix. It is essential that the matrix be adapted to match the assessments used by the teachers in a given school or jurisdiction. What we have provided here is just one example that is the result of working with jurisdictions and schools over the past 10 years. Once this is done, teachers are able to use the matrix to group their students for small-group instruction without delay. We have seen the process of moving from assessment to instruction shortened by as much as six weeks; within a week, teachers know their students well enough to start effectively grouping them with greater efficiency beyond a single text or phonics measure.

The Student Learning Profile and the Instructional Strategies Matrix are tools to assist teachers as they create instructional groups and initiate instruction that is focused on student learning needs. However, the purpose of a CLIP is to ensure that teaching *continues* to be focused on a daily basis. The tool for achieving this is the previously described Focus Sheet. As teachers select indicators relevant to the stage reached by individuals and plan their teaching accordingly, they also monitor on a daily basis the progress of students as they instruct them in small-group settings in which students can readily be observed. Let us consider what the Focus Sheet might look like for Tanya's Grade 1 group at the beginning of the second week of instruction (Figure 5.8).

In this example, the session consists of a one-hour reading block and a 30-minute skills block in which the class works as a whole to review and acquire the necessary phonemic awareness and phonics and vocabulary skills to support both reading and writing. The teacher begins with 15 minutes of whole-class instruction devoted to Shared Reading. The teacher selects the text for the Shared Reading to illustrate the indicators (teaching foci) that he or she wants to reinforce or introduce during this lesson. By selecting a three-foci approach to Shared Reading, the teacher can take into account the range of performance levels within the class. Each focus is an opportunity to gear the instruction toward a particular group of students rather than simply proceeding with the average student in mind, which is so often the case in whole-class instruction. When teachers have the pretest information for all students and an individual Student Learning Profile for each student, they can make these more focused decisions within the context of whole-class instruction (see Crévola & Vineis, 2004a, for more detail).

Figure 5.8.   Sample Focus Sheet

FOCUS SHEET: READING K–3		
Class: *1C*		Date: *9/28*

Whole Class

Title: *Growing Mushrooms*

Teaching Focuses:
1. *Formulate responses based on personal experiences*
2. *Use picture clues to assist with unfamiliar words*
3. *Produce a phrased and fluent reading*

Small Group

Group1 **Instructional Strategy:** ❑ Oral Language ❑ Language Experience ❑ Shared Reading ❑ Guided Reading ❑ Reciprocal Teaching	Materials: *Item* Title: *Planting a Garden* Text Level: *E*	Students	Tonya A.	David C.	Carlos E.	Sam G.	Marcie H.	Chung K.
Foci:	1. *Formulates responses to author's message based on personal experiences, beliefs, and understandings of the world*		✓	✓	✓	✗	✓	✓
	2. *Use a variety of strategies such as beginning, middle, and final letters, spelling patterns, word endings, etc., to problem-solve on unfamiliar words*		✗	✗	✓	✓	✓	✗

Comments for Future Instruction:

Tanya, David, and Chung all need more work in using a variety of strategies at the word level. Sara will benefit from staying in this group. Provide extra opportunities in learning centers to have these students work on Vocabulary and word-attack skills. Select another nonfiction text for a Read To in small group session.

Whole Class

Share Focus:
Articulate what you learned today that will help you as a reader
Comments for Future Instruction:
Need to make sure to allocate a share focus to students who are needing practice articulating their learning

In this example, the 15 minutes of whole-class instruction is followed by 40 minutes of independent and small-group work. During this time, the teacher takes two small instructional groups for

20 minutes each. Tanya has been grouped with five other students who are also Beginning readers. For this particular session, the teacher has selected two related indicators as the foci of instruction. The teacher uses the Focus Sheet to plan the instruction, including selecting the teaching foci and the students in each group. Immediately following the lesson, the teacher assesses how each student has progressed against the goals of the lesson and writes an evaluation of the lesson to inform future instruction and grouping.

Focus Sheets are written immediately following the previous lesson. There is no need for long-range planning in which teachers choose books days, weeks, and even months ahead of instruction. In this approach, while the middle-term goals of instruction are known well in advance, detailed lesson planning is possible only after instruction, which means that principals and district leaders would not require monthly or quarterly planners that designate lessons' content well ahead of the instruction and without a knowledge of students' progress and learning needs.

CLASSROOM ORGANIZATION

From the above example, it is clear that implementing the CLIP for early literacy depends very much on the effective use within classes of small instructional groups and a variety of powerful instructional strategies to provide focused teaching. Flexible and constantly changing small instructional groups allow teachers to teach to the needs of individual students but in a way that is much more efficient than individual conferencing.

In the context of early literacy instruction, individual conferencing is a highly effective teaching strategy, but it lacks the efficiency of small-group instruction. By teaching six to eight students in a small group rather than using individual conferences, a teacher can ensure that all students receive instruction focused on their needs more regularly. It must not be forgotten that narrowing the achievement gap and providing equal opportunities for all students is not the same as providing equal time to all students. Some students need more time and more support. By providing daily short and focused small-group instruction times for the most at-risk students, teachers can improve their students' chances of success.

A considerable body of evidence indicates that substantial gains in student learning are possible if small-group instruction is used.

For example, in a meta-analysis of 103 independent studies (Abrami, Lou, Chambers, Poulsen, & Spence, 2000), it was found that there was an overall effect size of +0.17 of a standard deviation for small-group over whole-class teaching; the effect size increased massively when:

- outcomes were measured using locally developed rather than standardized tests
- teachers were provided with special training in small-group teaching
- grouping was based on ability as well as other considerations
- cooperative learning methods were used
- students were enrolled in lower elementary schools

When these conditions were in place, mean effect sizes of +1.17 (high ability), +1.01 (medium ability), and +0.96 (low ability) were observed. These are unusually large effects and justify the effort to overcome any obstacles encountered when seeking to implement small-group instruction in classrooms.

Over the past 10 years, the authors have worked with hundreds of schools to introduce small-group instruction as part of a comprehensive design approach to teaching early literacy in Australia and the United States. This experience has convinced us that small-group work is an indispensable element in the design of classroom literacy instruction that focuses precisely on the learning needs of all students. It has also underscored the importance of putting in place classroom management routines and of designing activities that allow small-group instruction to proceed without disruption from the rest of the class. As mentioned earlier, teachers typically need assistance and encouragement in setting up task management boards, time clocks, book baskets, table organizers, and transition routines to ensure that students are able to operate productively when the teacher is engaged in small-group instruction. In a fully developed CLIP, we envision including a teachers' handbook that would deal specifically with all aspects of classroom management and organization relevant to implementing the CLIP. Crévola and Vineis (2004a) have provided some general guidance for the successful implementation of the initial phase of a CLIP. The work of Carol Ann Tomlinson (1998), which has long been a staple resource for teachers and schools seeking to implement a more individually tailored instructional program, is also highly relevant. Tomlinson has provided guidance on the practicalities of establishing a differentiated program and on associated classroom management issues.

LOOPS AND DETOURS IN THE CRITICAL LEARNING INSTRUCTIONAL PATH

In constructing a CLIP, the focus is necessarily on the path taken by the *average* learner. While learners may have different starting points and proceed at different rates, most do indeed broadly follow the same path to becoming literate. Some, however, will not be able to make progress by sticking to the main path. For these students, loops or detours are needed to address their particular needs and help them to get back on track as quickly as possible. Unfortunately, many practices that ostensibly seek to deal with individual differences in readiness either create or perpetuate inequalities and do not help students catch up.

There are no hard and fast rules about these detours. What we can be sure about is that those who develop checklists of milestones based on average patterns of performance will always find that some students have great difficulty with some areas and little difficulty with others. Marie Clay (1998) offers the following advice in responding to these situations:

Teachers who try to find out what children do not know (and much testing is directed to this) are looking for initial points of contact in the wrong places. What they need to do is find points of contact in children's prior learning, the things that children *can* do, and spend a little time helping children firm up their grasp of what they already know. (p. 3)

Teachers understandably worry about students who defy their best efforts to educate. We do not at this stage know all that we would like to know about the factors that prevent many children from making progress. While the field of reading abounds with magic cures, the evidence regarding their effectiveness is often lacking or disconfirming. In the absence of proven solutions, Clay's (1998) advice that we should seek to build on what students do know and can do remains powerful. In other words, it is not so much a question of *constructing* loops or detours when we don't know where they are taking us, but rather *following and supporting* the students who make them and assisting them in regaining the main path as quickly as possible.

BEYOND EARLY LITERACY

To make the notion of a CLIP as concrete as possible, we have done so with reference to early literacy for students ages 4.5 to 8 years (K–3). In fact, our focus has been even narrower, as it has been confined to reading. It is now time to consider the relevance of our proposed approach to other areas of the curriculum and to other levels of schooling.

We are in no doubt that CLIPs can be developed in a range of curriculum areas spanning all levels of schooling, and we hope this will happen. We caution, however, that the CLIP approach has greatest relevance for areas that are critical in the sense that they involve essential knowledge that all students need to acquire, such as mathematics and science. We are frankly doubtful about CLIPs' relevance in areas such as music or visual arts, and we are uncertain as to how one might proceed in a content-rich subject such as high school history.

However, middle school mathematics would be a good example of an area of the curriculum that we believe is ripe for Breakthrough thinking along the lines illustrated for early literacy. Of course, adaptations would be needed to fit the subject and the ages of the students. For example, instead of breaking the journey into key stages, which makes sense for early literacy, topics or key ideas such as Place Value, Percentages, or Ratio make much more sense for middle school mathematics. The ordering of these topics or key ideas is not so critical as the ordering of key stages in early literacy, but within a given topic or key idea, there is likely to be a strict hierarchy or sequencing of indicators.

Regarding the indicators of progress, much work has been done in recent years to provide teachers with fine-grained descriptions that allow daily tracking of students' growth as they develop in their understanding of mathematics. A good example is *Concept Book: A Mathematics Reference for Teachers and Students* (America's Choice, 2005), which has been conceived as a reference that belongs in the hands not only of the teacher but also of the student, thus enabling students to play a more active role in regulating their own learning.

Another adaptation would be in class grouping practices and forms of classroom organization appropriate to middle school mathematics. For example, there might be less emphasis on small-group instruction and a greater emphasis on students working in pairs. But the core ideas remain the same:

1. A set of powerful and aligned assessment tools tied to the learning objectives of each lesson that give the teacher access to accurate and comprehensive information on the progress of each student on a daily basis and that can be administered without unduly interrupting normal classroom routines

2. A method to allow the formative assessment data to be captured in a way that is not time-consuming, to analyze the data automatically, to convert it into information that is powerful enough to drive instructional decisions not sometime in the future, but tomorrow

3. A means of using the assessment information on each student to design and implement personalized instruction; assessment for learning is a strategy for improving instruction in precise ways

4. A built-in means of monitoring and managing learning, of testing what works, and of systematically improving the effectiveness of classroom instruction so that it more precisely responds to the learning needs of each student in the class

It is to the last of these four ideas that we now turn.

LOCKING IN ONGOING IMPROVEMENT

Inevitably, any CLIP will initially have shortcomings and should be treated as an initial hypothesis to be tested and as a set of processes and procedures that need to be improved gradually through attention to design. It is thus important that the data generated through implementing the CLIP be collected and systematically analyzed and evaluated and that there be mechanisms for updating the critical path and for making ongoing improvements to processes and procedures. This is, after all, what the whole notion of improvement by design is all about.

At the level of the individual student, CLIPs mean that a detailed and constantly updated profile of performance is available that traces the individual's learning over several years of schooling. There is thus a complete history (which teachers constructed on a day-to-day basis) of when and where the individual experienced problems or enjoyed success and what the instructional response was. On the basis of this information, individual learning plans can be generated for *all* students and not just those who are falling significantly behind their peers. Like a person's medical records, such histories mean that successive teachers of the same child do not start ignorant of their students but with complete and up-to-date records that enable them to plan instruction with confidence. Student histories also facilitate communication with parents and caregivers, who can be given precise information about the child's progress and advice on how they can support the child's learning.

At the level of the class, a CLIP allows the performance of whole classes of students to be monitored. Support can be directed more readily to those classes in which students are making little progress because the data will indicate both whether and when instruction was provided and whether and when it was effective. Critical paths should not be allowed to become a tool for teacher surveillance and control, but they should facilitate targeted support of teachers in improving the quality of their classroom instruction.

At the level of the system, when a CLIP is implemented in a large number of schools, data are generated that facilitate more targeted support to individual schools as well as support to address common problems identified across all schools. It is rare to find a school system that is driven by knowledge of the daily progress of the students in its schools and that accepts responsibility for creating the conditions under which teachers and school administrators can best promote student learning. As we have discussed earlier, it is precisely this degree of alignment and focus that is needed. CLIPs can generate the information that can transform systems and enable them to concentrate on their core business of improving learning.

Finally, at a macro level, we might see a CLIP implemented across many school systems, thus creating the opportunity to use the data from large numbers of classrooms to update and improve the critical path and the structures and resources that support it. More important, the opportunity exists to engage in a systematic program of design-based research and experimentation. As noted in Chapter 4, we see this as central to transforming classroom instruction into an expert, scientifically based activity that provides precision, not prescription.

BUILDING THE SYSTEM

At this stage, the reader might well be asking whether we have not missed a crucial step. How did the data arising from pre- and posttesting of students, together with teachers' daily use of focus sheets in planning and monitoring instruction, become available for use in the ways envisaged in the preceding section? As we all know, it is not a simple matter to establish and sustain systematic, data-driven approaches to classroom instruction because of the logistical problems involved, particularly the problem of capturing and recording the information in the hectic, messy, and technologically primitive environments of most classrooms and schools.

All of the tools that we have described thus far can be found in various degrees of sophistication in classrooms, mostly in hard-copy format. These tools need to be brought together and integrated into expert instructional systems in which the hard work is taken out of the task of collecting and using the data. Such a system would integrate all of the components needed to implement the CLIP.

Figure 5.9 indicates some of the key components that would constitute the architecture of such a system. At the heart of the system would be four components. The *Database* would contain the updated information on students, their progress and other relevant classroom, school, and systems characteristics. The *Knowledge Base* would contain the critical path itself, the teaching strategies, the available resources, and other relevant information including supporting research evidence, answers to frequently asked questions, and so on.

The role of the *Inference System* would be to constantly interrogate both the Database and the Knowledge Base, largely through a series of *if-then* algorithms, to provide teachers, coaches, principals, system administrators, and project staff the information and expert advice they need. This would take the form of a series of preformatted or user-generated reports. Critically, for the classroom teacher, it would generate a suggested Focus Sheet for the next lesson indicating:

- the suggested instructional foci
- the number and composition of small instructional groups
- the suggested teaching strategies to be used
- the resources available to the teacher

Figure 5.9.   Components of the Instructional System

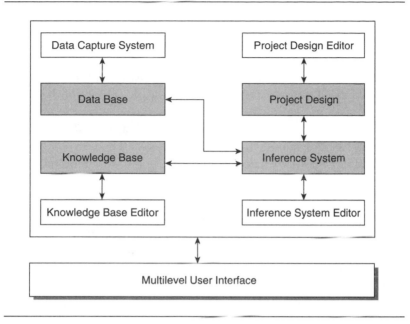

Of course, this would still leave much to the professional judgment of teachers, and instruction itself would remain entirely in their hands. The precision is inserted by streamlining the organization of the data and generating appropriate instructional sequences.

The *Project Design Editor* would enable a project director to input information specifying how the CLIP is to be implemented in different classrooms. It could build in alternative paths to allow for different levels of experience and knowledge in using the system, thus allowing for phased implementation. It could also facilitate the management of design experiments in which specific elements of the CLIP are systematically varied in randomly selected classrooms.

A key component would be the *Data Capture System*. There are now many examples of excellent systems for capturing online pre- and posttest data generated by schools and districts. The tricky problem is capturing assessment information on a daily basis. Teachers are typically not provided with tablet PCs that are light and durable. This situation must and will change in the future. In the meantime, the best solution appears to be to use scanning technology to capture these data and to have a dedicated administrative assistant in each school who manages and maintains the database. This is cheap and quick and takes the teacher literally a few minutes each day but saves much more time in the long run by making teaching more precise and hence more efficient.

The most important component, as far as users are concerned, would be the *User Interface,* which would look different, have different functions, and provide controlled levels of access to information for different users (e.g., classroom teacher, coach/coordinator, principal, system administrator, and project staff).

Building such a system is a major task. Indeed, it could only be done through a rigorously planned and conducted, large-scale, and adequately resourced research and development effort. It would require high levels of investment and a partnership between publicly funded university research centers, school systems, and private companies with expertise in online testing and publishing. We are convinced, however, that only through such a concerted effort and partnership will the Breakthrough occur.

Building the system is the technical challenge. The more difficult challenge lies in bringing about the kinds of change in thinking and practice at the school and system level that are entailed in implementing CLIPs and in achieving a Breakthrough in thinking about classroom instruction. This will require Breakthrough leadership at all levels of the system, a topic to which we now turn.

NOTES

1. The notion of leveled texts is familiar to many teachers, whether it be via the A-R levels of Fountas & Pinnell (1996), empirically based leveling techniques such as the Lexiles Framework developed by MetaMetrics, Inc. (Stenner, 1996), or Reading Recovery levels 1–26.

2. That is, not previously used in small-group instruction.

3. Crévola first developed the idea for the Strategies Matrix and the Focus Sheet in 1998 while working with schools and teachers in the Children's Literacy Success Strategy (CLaSS) in Victoria, Australia, and also in the Building Essential Literacy (BEL). Crévola and Vineis (2004b) have since developed a Key Assessments Reading Stage Chart, similar to this matrix, as part of Mondo Publishing's New York Bookshop Reading Program.

CHAPTER SIX

Breakthrough Leadership

A Way Forward

I n this chapter, we start by briefly reminding the reader what is needed and where schools are in relation to the need, and then we spend the bulk of the time on Breakthrough leadership across the system as a solution. Using our knowledge about how to bring about successful change on a large scale will be critical to this ambitious endeavor.

WHAT IS NEEDED

We have already outlined the nature of focused teaching, but we underscore here its essential meaning so that we can backward-map toward the kind of leadership infrastructure that will be necessary to reap Breakthrough results.

Yes, personalization is basic, and yes, greater precision in serving each student's learning needs is required, but the turnkey to these twin developments is *daily* professional learning on the part of every teacher. The classroom is key. Much lip service and considerable policy action have been directed at the importance of having a quality teacher in every classroom, but in our view, very few policymakers, or practitioners for that matter, really understand what quality means on a daily basis. Quality is not about a set of static characteristics or traits but about practices that need to be refined and extended every day. So Point 1 is that policymakers and educators need to understand what it means to be a learning teacher.

Point 2 is that ongoing learning for individuals paradoxically is, above all, *relational*. If schools combine these two components—daily, relational learning—they will soon realize that all learning that counts involves learning in context, that is, continuous improvement within the settings where we work. When one learns in context, two potentially beneficial things happen: The learning is by definition specific to the situation at hand; and it is, again by definition, shared.

Of course, one can learn nothing *new* in given settings or learn it superficially or even learn the wrong thing—worse still, without knowing that this is the case. Few people realize what focused instruction for every student really means on a daily basis. A careful reading of Chapters 3 through 5 reveals that teachers will need continuous learning opportunities to get that good.

We can also get a sense of what will be needed by considering the experiences of teachers who do deeply learn new instructional strategies. In a major study of the implementation of new mathematics and science policies in Michigan, Spillane (2004) found that teachers who substantially changed their teaching were intensely supported by close-to-instruction interaction with other teachers and external experts. As he observes,

> Day-to-day classroom practice was a core element of professional development [we would say professional learning]. Knowledge about instruction . . . was not a commodity imported from the outside into a classroom, [but rather] it was constructed through conversations among teachers, administrators, and external experts. The curriculum for teacher professional development was spread across students' work, national standards, classroom curriculum materials, and teachers' attempts to implement the standards in their practice . . . teachers' motivation to learn and change involved developing and sustaining teachers' identities as experts and learners with one another. (pp. 60–61)

Spillane (2004) shows that sustained engagement with an idea is critical for deep conceptual change and that such understanding takes years rather than months to acquire. Furthermore, Spillane found that sustained learning opportunities for teachers depend on leadership and coordination at the school and district levels. The problem he found was that this occurred in very few settings, affecting not much more than 10 percent of the teachers (and even then, one would expect that these conditions did not prevail over time). The vast majority of teachers never got to learn beyond the surface level.

The main difference between Spillane's (2004) research and our proposal is that he was focusing on "the latest innovation," whereas we are talking about transforming the system so that teachers are always learning. In this sense, the notion of the latest innovation fades as new ideas are built into daily interactions inside and outside the school.

To sum up, teachers need refined and focused knowledge all the time. It is a never-ending proposition. Mere information (of which teachers have a glut) gets transformed into knowledge through interaction, and knowledge becomes wisdom through sustained interaction. Teachers, thus, become experts over time, but only under these conditions.

Two synergistic purposes are served in the processes just described—deeper and more precise *knowledge* is continually being generated; and at the same time, *motivation* to push further is constantly being fueled. Because the system is highly interactive, knowledge and motivation not only become fused but also come to have the indispensable quality of being *shared*. This means the power of social capital is being used in the service of learning for all.

Schools need a systemic solution, and for this, they will need to draw on both their knowledge about how to manage change and what is known about instruction. The glue that links them is leadership. We start with change knowledge.

Using Change Knowledge

Our growing knowledge base and recent experience about what it takes to achieve successful large-scale reform are key reasons why we are optimistic that the field of education is close to a new tipping point. We have recently advocated (Barber & Fullan, 2005; Fullan, 2005) a Tri-Level Reform Solution—what has to happen at the:

1. school and community level

2. district/regional level

3. state/federal level

We first summarize 10 conclusions arising from this work.

1. The vast majority of teachers are motivated by moral purpose when ideas for activating it are evident.

2. People begin to change their behaviors before they change their beliefs. New positive experiences are the motivator, especially when they relate to fulfilling moral purpose.

3. Shared vision and ownership are less a precondition for success than they are an *outcome* of a quality process. Successful systems build vision and ownership through the quality of their learning processes and corresponding results.

4. Learning in context is key. Even the best professional-development workshops represent only input for success. Actual success occurs in the context of daily learning.

5. Professional learning communities at the school level are crucial in establishing cultures in which teachers learn from each other and school leaders and teachers collaborate for continuous improvement.

6. Professional learning communities will not be sustained unless the district and other levels of the system actively foster and maintain their development.

7. Districts and states must integrate pressure and support so that everyone within the system seriously engages in capacity building with a focus on results. Capacity building is what most policymakers neglect. Capacity building involves the use of strategies that increase the collective effectiveness of all levels of the system in developing and mobilizing knowledge, resources, and motivation, all of which are needed to raise the bar and close the gap of student learning across the system.

8. Lateral capacity building is crucial for spreading knowledge and increasing commitment. Lateral capacity building consists of strategies that enable schools to learn from each other—districts, states, and even countries learn from each other, too.

9. Leadership is the turnkey to system transformation. This means leaders working with a Breakthrough focus and doing so through the development of other leaders as they go.

10. It doesn't matter where the change starts as long as it is systemic thereafter. And systemic means a focus on establishing expert instructional systems that serve the needs of all levels.

The above conclusions point to a set of underlying components of effective change, all of which are required because they feed on each other in a positive spiral. The good news is that we see many instances where these components are in place at all three levels of our tri-level solution. Several school districts that we and others are working with are moving down the pathway of systemic reform. Increasingly, government policy leaders are gravitating toward capacity building as they realize that current strategies are not getting them anywhere on a large scale. At the same time, there are all too many instances of systems in which these characteristics are absent. In many states of the United States, No Child Left Behind is falling painfully short of its goals. The Breakthrough aspirations are there, but there is no focused strategy for capacity building (or even a recognition that one would be needed). In these states, No Child Left Behind cannot succeed until there is a new understanding of the need for capacity building.

Similarly, efforts to turn failing schools around are being narrowly conceived. In examining turnaround policies and strategies in different countries, Michael Fullan concluded that the strategies not only are excessively narrow and short sighted but also actually establish conditions that virtually guarantee unsustainability. Breakthrough solutions are much more fundamental and must be both systemic and explicitly and powerfully focused on raising the bar and closing the gap. Not doing that exacerbates the pernicious and pervasive personal and social consequences of failing in a high-performance context (Fullan, 2006).

In sum, and on balance, although significant ill-conceived policies and strategies persist, a great deal of knowledge and many ideas are available for getting it right. Our Tri Level Solution requires that this knowledge be put into practice by Breakthrough leadership at all levels of the system.

THE BREAKTHROUGH FRAMEWORK

In Chapter 1, we noted that external accountability systems do not take into account the need to develop internal accountability in the school and the district. We quoted Elmore (2004) as saying that schools can't respond to external accountability pressures when all questions of accountability related to student learning are essentially questions of individual teacher responsibility. Currently, principals, district leaders, and system leaders are in a weak position to take responsibility for the quality of instruction because they have so little real information on what is taught, let alone how well.

Given the instructional system outlined in Chapter 4, school leaders are placed in a very different position. There can be real-time monitoring of what is taught and how students are progressing. Just as the hospital management had no idea how to control costs and improve the quality of care before the advent of critical care pathways, so principals and school leaders currently lack the tools and the information for improving the precision and hence the effectiveness and efficiency of teaching.

With the tools and with the data described in Chapter 5, school leaders no longer have to wait until the end of the year (by which time it is too late) to find out whether learning outcomes improved. Rather, data would be available on a *daily* basis. This means that school leaders can immediately identify the students who need extra assistance and exactly what kind of help they need. They can promptly identify those classrooms in which the pace of instruction is falling behind or proceeding too fast, or in which students are making slow or rapid progress. This means school leaders can provide targeted support to teachers rather than playing the blame game when it's too late to change the outcome. More important, school leaders have the data to identify common problems and concerns and to lead inquiry into how the instructional system could be improved.

This opens up the prospect of a new kind of instructional leadership in which school and district leaders are not always operating in the dark and without good information about what is actually going on in each classroom and school. In these new circumstances, there can be real internal accountability and empowerment of superintendents and principals to lead and manage instruction in an informed and proactive manner.

It will take a powerful framework to enable this new kind of leadership and a push from all quarters to take schools beyond the current tipping point. This is a feasible proposition, given the action now under way. Figure 6.1 contains our recommendation for how schools can approach this exciting new Breakthrough. We first

Figure 6.1.   Breakthrough Framework

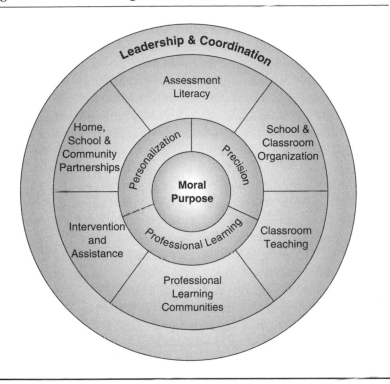

provide an overview of the framework and then move to the implications for leadership.

As Figure 6.1 shows, there are three inner core functions, namely our Triple P model—personalization, precision, and professional learning. Six core functions support the three Ps: assessment literacy, school and classroom organization, classroom teaching, professional learning communities, intervention and assistance, and home and school/community partnerships. Finally, there are leadership and coordination across the three levels of schools, districts, and the state that are required to orchestrate the first two layers.

No one is near making this system work across the three levels, but there are many valuable pieces available in our metaphorical corporate basement ready for creative recombination (Abrahamson, 2004). Our efforts involving the Victoria (Australia) Catholic schools and with York Region in Ontario are two such examples, and there are many others. What is needed now is proactive leadership in which individuals and groups seek ways of connecting to adjacent layers of the system. In the end, distributive leadership will make it work. Such leadership does not involve dividing leadership responsibilities or delegating them but rather seeing leadership coalesce around focused instruction. The model is decidedly relational and requires permeable connectivity. As we have written elsewhere, everyone needs to be a leader, and leaders from all levels must be engaged in changing the context as a whole. These are our "system thinkers in action" (Fullan, 2005).

We can outline the main functions, and then educational leaders will need to work up examples that indeed are systemic. The inner core of the system is our Triple P model. Moral purpose, continuous best practice, and education for all constitute the core work of schools in each and every classroom.

For this to work requires the six functions in the third ring of the Breakthrough framework. This represents the content of the expert system. We know what much of this looks like because the functions have been implemented at the school and district levels (Hill & Crévola, 1999). We need to remind the reader of Senge's (1990) system criterion—the model will not work if any one of the components is missing or underperforming.

Assessment literacy encompasses standards, targets, and the use of data to inform instruction through assessment for and of learning. Standards and targets represent expectations for student achievement and need to be reflected in explicit standards that have been benchmarked against those of other schools and school systems to ensure that they reflect effective practice. Standards and associated targets constitute the starting point for redesigning how schools operate so that meeting the standards comes first in everything that schools do. Such standards need not and should not be imposed from the top. Although doing so is complex, standards and targets need to be negotiated across the three levels, and above all, they must continually be informed by the other five functions.

In addition to standards and targets, assessment literacy includes the use of assessment data to drive instruction. All leaders need to be able to cycle back and forth between using information to refine instruction and engaging in external discussion of how well they are doing. Teaching and learning involves regular monitoring and assessment of students. The design of this element needs to be such as to ensure that consistent, coherent information is generated on a regular basis on the progress of all students and on all key indicators. Assessment is important to determine whether targets have been met. Effective teachers closely monitor their students' progress so that they can ensure that each student is always working within his or her level of challenge. Indeed, the most important function of monitoring and assessment is to assist the teacher to develop a profile for each student, to establish starting points for teaching, and to use this diagnostic information to drive classroom instruction. Thus, educators need to be experts in assessment both *of* and *for* learning vis-à-vis standards and targets.

School and class organization involves establishing and continually refining conditions conducive to providing explicit support for focused instruction. To maximize engaged learning time and to facilitate teaching that is responsive to student needs, interests, and current readiness to learn, organizational structures and processes within the school must be aligned. For example, it is important to ensure that adequate time is devoted to key learning outcomes and that this time is, as far as possible, free from interruptions. In large schools, it is important that structures are in place that promote cohesion, pastoral care, and a sense of identity, structures that do not lead to feelings of isolation and alienation among students. It is also important that classroom organization facilitates focused teaching. School and district leaders need to be aware of the findings of research into such issues as the impact of class size and of different forms of school and class organization, including within-class student grouping practices. These are issues that impinge massively on the resources available within schools and on the capacity of teachers to focus their teaching on the needs, aptitudes, and abilities of their students.

Classroom teaching strategies consist of effective teaching that is structured and focused on the learning needs of each student in the class. It requires teachers to have detailed understandings of how children learn; well-developed classroom routines, structures, organization, and management; and the ability to motivate and engage students using a range of classroom practices and strategies.

Professional learning communities must exist within the school, but we also use the term to refer to all learning that will be required through relationships with other schools, the district, state personnel, and professional networks. Capacity building of the system requires lateral and vertical learning relationships. A crucial element in any design aimed at improved teaching and learning in schools is the provision of effective, ongoing, and professional learning opportunities for teachers, opportunities that promote learning not just of individuals but of the organization and system as a whole. Put another way, central to a design approach to improving learning in schools is the establishment of a culture and of systems and processes for promoting organizational learning. Professional learning groups function through a mixture of both off- and on-campus learning but principally through a combination of demonstration teaching, mentoring, coaching, and opportunities for the team to debrief and reflect on teachers' practice and progress.

Intervention and assistance are required when, even with the best classroom teaching in place, many students fail to make satisfactory progress. Among these students will be those with disabilities, those who come from homes devoid of books and families that see no purpose in school learning, those who may have severe emotional blocks that interfere with their concentration, and those who are transient or who may have frequent absences from school. For such students, the school will need to establish systems and processes that provide support and assistance beyond regular classroom instruction to enable them to catch up quickly to their peers. Without timely and effective intervention, these students fall further and further behind in their schoolwork and experience diminished self-esteem and increased alienation from schooling. For the lowest-achieving students, one-to-one or very small group instruction is likely to be the only way to bring them to standard and transform them into motivated and engaged learners.

Home, school, and community partnerships involve linking with the home, with feeder schools, and with the community; they are important at all levels of schooling. A strong body of research shows that students make greater progress when parents, caregivers, and the community are supportive of the work of the school and involved in its activities. But for school to be effective, it is not enough to establish links with the home: What are needed are comprehensive and permanent programs of partnerships with families and communities. We have found that when teachers and the school as a whole become more effective at what they are doing, they increasingly reach out to the community, seeing external partners as a vital part of the solution. It seems that when teachers are less effective, they take fewer risks and play it safe by staying behind the classroom door, thereby aggravating the problem.

Breakthrough Leadership

The outer ring of the Breakthrough framework refers to the kind of leadership and coordination needed for the system to have a chance of being established. Success will depend on strategies that foster leadership at all levels of the system. It will depend on leaders who are able to develop yet other leaders, who together form a critical mass of interacting and coalescing leadership for change across the three levels of the system—school, district, and state (Fullan, 2005).

School Leadership

The more the system we describe gets established, the more every teacher becomes a leader because teachers will operate as interactive expert learners all the time. To progress, especially in the early stages, the principal is key, along with at least one other internal change agent (we oversimplify here, but the so-called second change agent, such as a literacy coordinator, is essential for staying on focus). Studies of effective schools have consistently drawn attention to the importance of strong educational leadership. Good teaching may be possible in a school in which there is weak and ineffective educational leadership, but it is harder to achieve. Change and sustained improvement are impossible without good educational leadership, particularly where whole-school change is sought. Educational leadership and coordination, as we have said, are not the sole responsibility of school principals: They can and should be exercised at all levels of the organization. In particular, attention has been drawn to the critical role of lead teachers who are given release time that enables them to coordinate and lead professional learning teams and act as mentors, coaches, and lead learners. It is nevertheless incumbent on principals to ensure that leadership and coordination are indeed happening at all levels and that they are allocating sufficient time to the role, relative to other roles, such as administration, the management of personnel, student welfare issues, and so on.

In addition to intraschool support, our model requires that school leaders be dynamically plugged into the external expert system. Schools have a moral and intellectual responsibility to learn from other schools and agencies and to contribute what they know to others. Some of the most powerful learning (and enhanced moral commitments) that we have witnessed has come from lateral capacity-building relationships among clusters of schools working together over time.

All of this is a tall order, and we have already suggested that the new role of the principal will require substantial revamping on the part of the system. Presently, the role is encumbered by excess baggage and far too many demands and distractions from the main teaching and learning mission of the school. There is considerable agreement that the principal is key, but there is also a system failure to act on this belief. Our recommendation is that districts and states reexamine the principal's role with a view to reducing the distractors, mainly by figuring out how management and administrative duties can be addressed more efficiently. We do not envisage a wholesale restructuring solution. That would be a waste of resources. Rather, we favor tackling the problem on the ground by shifting the center of gravity of the principal's work as school leader so that it is increasingly focused on implementing the agenda in Figure 6.1. Future principals will have to know a great deal more about teaching and learning and associated support systems than they currently do.

Within the school, then, the role of leadership is to help provide the focus and expert support system for all teachers with an emphasis on what is needed to personalize each classroom with greater instructional precision. This must be done while fostering strong connections and relationships with other parts of the system. Although the primary focus must be on the classroom, school staff also have a responsibility to be aware of issues and responsibilities vis-à-vis the larger system. We agree with Heifetz and Linsky (2002) that effective leaders need to have the capacity to be simultaneously on the dance floor and in the balcony. This is how systems change.

District Leadership

Just as the principal needs to ensure leadership and coordination with teachers, the role of the district is to help cause whole-system change, that is, moving toward the future where all schools operate within and across the district according to the principles we have outlined. Moreover, as with all of our Breakthrough leadership, districts must pay attention to the work of other districts and to state policymakers. We have worked in districts ranging from three schools to more than 600. Clearly, the details of Breakthrough vary according to size. Very small districts must form learning relationships with other districts. Larger ones must subdivide into clusters, being careful that clusters do not become isolated.

In all cases, the district has a mediating role between schools and the state. In particular, the district's role can be interpreted through the lens of Figure 6.1. The centerpiece involves forming the moral mission of all schools, all classrooms, in relation to personalization, precision, and professional learning. There is a major role in recruiting, retaining, and developing teachers and other leaders in the system— getting and keeping the right people on the bus and in the right seats. A system of distributed leadership—one in which the role of leaders is seen both as fostering a focus on teaching and learning and as developing other leaders who can go even further—is essential.

The district influences schools through the six functions in Figure 6.1. It clarifies standards and negotiates targets as part of a tri-level system (school, district, state). The district has a substantial role in providing resources and setting up a state-of-the-art assessment system. Assessment of and for learning depends crucially on the right information being available in a timely manner, much of it on a daily basis. The district must also figure out, with school leaders, the right apparatus and modus operandi of school teams and the interaction of schools with each other as they go about capacity building through professional learning communities, identifying classroom practices that serve different learning needs, and making head- way on the difficult but critical issue of forming partnerships with parents and communities. And the district must be prepared to inter- vene when certain schools are not able to meet the learning needs of all of their students.

The external face of districts involves being an active player, learning from and contributing to the development of other districts, and being part of two-way traffic concerning state policy and per- formance of the system as a whole. Again, there is much already under way in the countries with which we are familiar. It is a matter of building on these promising starts, both to go deeper and to spread the best ideas to other districts.

There are already well-developed examples of districts moving in this direction (see Sharratt & Fullan, in press). While we have stressed that professional learning must occur for every teacher and for every principal, make no mistake about it—such learning in context cannot happen unless district leadership engages all schools in this joint journey.

State Leadership and Other Big Players

We take up here the role of the state as the main policy entity, not delving into the intricacies of federal/state relationships in those jurisdictions that have such distinctions. Whatever the structure, our main points remain. Just as teachers cannot move forward as a group without school and district leadership, districts and systems cannot advance without new state/federal leadership. As we said before, the attraction is that the ideas we are proposing are working—they work morally because they get results; and because they get results, they work politically.

Over the past two decades, the state has become an increasingly prominent player, unfortunately with a one-sided focus on external accountability. We agree with Elmore (2004) that there can be no effective external accountability unless it is accompanied with internal (to the school and district) accountability. Our model basically builds up the internal capacity of schools to be effective and accountable.

What follows from this is that state policymakers and senior civil servants need to think and act differently and need to surround themselves with other leaders who can help do this. The incentive is considerable because most leaders know that the current system is not working (i.e., the policies being pursued are not working), and most have a strong interest in improving the public school system for a variety of economic and social health and well-being reasons. The severe social consequences of failing to address economic and education gaps between the highest and lowest performers have not been appreciated by policymakers and educators who focus only on the latest innovations or narrow intervention schemes. Large gaps go to the heart of societal health and prospects for the future of democracy itself (Fullan, 2006). As more examples get under way, government leaders can also learn from their peers in other jurisdictions who are attempting Breakthrough reforms. People learn best from their peers. Why should it be any different for elected officials and senior bureaucrats?

State leaders would be well advised to backward-map from our starting point—the solution lies in each and every classroom and depends on a system in which each teacher learns every day.

This means that policies and resources must be aimed at getting the elements in Figure 6.1 operating in harmony:

- Clarify standards and negotiate targets in a way that district and school leaders understand and own them—we hasten to remind the readers that any one of the elements does not stand alone and indeed is served by the other five functions being active in combination.
- Allocate resources for establishing strong assessment systems that serve assessment both for and of learning. There are few higher-yield strategies than investing in assessment literacy on a large scale.
- Direct policies and allocate resources that result in a system of innovation in relation to assessment practices, classroom teaching strategies, and home and school partnerships.
- Support districts in their quest to develop strong leadership at the local level, built around moral purpose and professional learning.
- Intervene in school and district situations where students are not being served.

Our model is based on a quid pro quo proposition. The state needs to do its part, as above, and as it does so, it has the right to expect that the other levels will reciprocate. Although we don't recommend that any level wait for another level to get its act together, in the long run, sustainable systems run on quid pro quo synergy. The idea is to create conditions that get all of the excuses off the table and then to expect results.

The state is also in a position to influence and connect with other big players, including business, foundations, universities, professional associations, and not-for-profit organizations, all of them having a critical role to play in moving toward the tipping point in creating a transformed educational system. In Chapter 4, we commented in particular on the need for a shift in thinking about the role of educational research and the need for more design-based research to develop and test the kinds of instructional systems that can support focused teaching and deliver personalized instruction. States can use funding to promote greater involvement of the research community in large-scale research and development efforts to create Breakthrough instructional systems.

CONCLUSION

As we said at the outset, our purpose in writing this book is partly to provide affirmation, encouragement, and new ideas to those schools, districts, and states already going down the Triple P pathway. For some, it would not take much to achieve the Breakthrough results we are advocating. Many are close enough that Breakthrough is a real possibility over the next decade. For others not so inclined (yet), we wanted to provide compelling ideas to encourage them to take this agenda seriously, to look into what they could do to get the step changes they so badly need but do not realize. Our prediction is that those who test these waters will find many takers toiling away in the corporate basements of our nations. It is not as if schools need to start from scratch; much of the groundwork has already been done.

A quantum breakthrough in public schooling is tantalizingly close. Nothing, and we mean nothing, is more critical to the future of the world than rapidly and constantly improving systems of public schooling that serve all students. Schools are as close as they have ever been to realizing this fantastic goal.

Every now and then, as the poet Seamus Heaney said, "hope and history rhyme." We don't know whether this is really such a time, but we are convinced that schools could with reasonable effort *make* them rhyme. It takes a whole village to raise one child, but it takes a system to raise *every* child. Breakthrough is about raising a system.

References

Abrahamson, E. (2004). *Change without pain*. Boston: Harvard Business School Press.

Abrami, P. C., Lou, Y., Chambers, C., Poulsen, C., & Spence, J. C. (2000). Why should we group students within-class for learning? *Educational Research and Evaluation, 6*(2), 158–179.

America's Choice. (2005). *Concept book: A mathematics reference for teachers and students*. Washington, DC: Author.

Barber, M., & Fullan, M. (2005, March 2). Tri-level development: It's the system. *Education Week,* pp. 15–16

Black, P., & Wiliam, D. (1998a). Assessment and classroom learning. *Assessment in Education, 5*(1), 7–74.

Black, P., & Wiliam, D. (1998b, October). Inside the black box: Raising standards through classroom assessment. *Phi Delta Kappan, 80*(2), 139–148.

Borman, G. D., Hewes, G. M., Overman, L. T., & Brown, S. (2003). Comprehensive school reform and achievement: A meta-analysis. *Review of Educational Research, 73*(2), 125–230.

Borman, K., & Associates (2005). *Meaningful urban education reform*. Albany: State University of New York Press.

Burkhardt, H., & Schoenfeld, A. H. (2003). Improving educational research: Toward a more useful, more influential, and better-funded enterprise. *Educational Researcher, 32*(9), 3–14.

Burney, D. (2004). Craft knowledge: The road to transforming schools. *Phi Delta Kappan, 85*(7), 526–532.

Carroll, J. B. (1989). The Carroll model: A 25-year retrospective and prospective view. *Educational Researcher, 18*(1), 26–31.

Clay, M. M. (1993). *Reading recovery: A guidebook for teachers in training*. Portsmouth, NH: Heinemann.

Clay, M. M. (1998). *By different paths to common outcomes*. York, ME: Stenhouse.

Cohen, D., & Hill, H. (2001). *Learning policy*. New Haven, CT: Yale University Press.

Cohen, D. K., Raudenbush, S. W., & Ball, D. L. (2003). Resources, instruction, and research. *Educational Evaluation and Policy Analysis, 25*(2), 119–142.

Cortazzi, M., & Jin Lixian. (2001). Large classes in China: "Good" teachers and interaction. In D. A. Watkins & J. B. Biggs (Eds.), *Teaching the Chinese learner: Psychological and pedagogical perspectives* (pp. 115–134). Hong Kong: University of Hong Kong, Comparative Education Research Centre.

Crévola, C. A., & Hill, P. W. (2000). *Children's literacy success strategy: An overview* (2nd ed.). Melbourne: Catholic Education Office.

Crévola, C., & Vineis, M. (2004a). *Building essential literacy with Bookshop: A research-based reading program.* New York: Mondo.

Crévola, C., & Vineis, M. (2004b). *Managing assessment and instruction: Grade 1.* New York: Mondo.

Cross City Campaign for Urban School Reform. (2005). *A delicate balance: District policies and classroom practice.* Chicago: Author.

Datnow, A., & Stringfield, S. (2000). Working together for reliable school reform. *Journal of Education for Students Placed at Risk, 5*(1), 183–204.

The Design-Based Research Collective. (2003). Design-based research: An emerging paradigm for educational inquiry. *Educational Researcher, 32*(1), 5–8.

Earl, L., Fullan, M., Leithwood, K., & Watson, N. (2003). *Watching & learning: OISE/UT evaluation of the national literacy and numeracy strategies.* London: Department for Education and Skills.

Elmore, R. F. (2004). *School reform from the inside out: Policy, practice, and performance.* Cambridge, MA: Harvard University Press.

Elmore, R. F., & McLaughlin, M. (1988). Steady work: Policy, practice, and the reform of American education. Santa Monica, CA: Rand.

Fielding, L., Kerr, N., & Rosier, P. (2004). *Delivering on the promise.* Kennewick, WA: The New Foundation Press.

Fountas, I. C., & Pinnell, G. S. (1996). *Guided reading: Good first teaching for all children.* Portsmouth, NH: Heinemann.

Fullan, M. (2005). *Leadership and sustainability.* Thousand Oaks, CA: Corwin.

Fullan, M. (2006). *Beyond turnaround leadership.* San Francisco: Jossey-Bass.

Gladwell, M. (2000). *The tipping point: How little things can make a big difference.* New York and Boston: Little, Brown.

Good, R. H., & Kaminski, R. A. (Eds.). (2002). *Dynamic indicators of basic early literacy skills* (6th ed.). Eugene, OR: Institute for the Development of Educational Achievement.

Hargreaves, A. (2003). *Teaching in the knowledge society.* New York: Teachers College Press.

Hargreaves, A., & Fink, D. (2006). *Sustainable leadership.* San Francisco: Jossey-Bass.

Hattie, J. A. (1999, June). *Influences on student learning.* Inaugural Professorial Address, University of Auckland.

Heifetz, R., & Linsky, M. (2002). *Leadership on the line.* Boston: Harvard Business School Press.

Hill, P. W., & Crévola, C. A. (1999). The role of standards in educational reform for the 21st century. In D. D. Marsh (Ed.), *ASCD Yearbook 1999: Preparing our schools for the 21st century* (pp. 117–142). Alexandria, VA: Association for Supervision and Curriculum Development.

Howe, I. (1969, February). Steady work. *Commentary, 47*(2).

Leadbeater, C. (2002). *Learning about personalization.* London: Innovation Unit, Department for Education and Skills.

Marzano, R. J. (2003). *What works in schools: Translating research into action.* Alexandria, VA: Association for Supervision and Curriculum Development.

Roos, B., & Hamilton, D. (2005). Formative assessment: A cybernetic viewpoint. *Assessment in Education, 12*(1), 7–20.

Sadler, D. R. (1989). Formative assessment in the design of instructional systems. *Instructional Science, 18,* 119–144.

Senge, P. (1990) *The fifth discipline.* New York: Doubleday.

Sergiovanni, T. J. (2000). Changing change: Towards a design science and art. *Journal of Educational Change, 1*(1), 57–75.

Scheerens. J., & Bosker, R. J. (1997). *The foundations of educational effectiveness.* Oxford, UK: Pergamon.

Sharratt, L., & Fullan. M. (in press). The school district that did the right things right. *Journal of School Leadership.*

Simon, H. A. (1996). *The sciences of the artificial: How schools misunderstand education policy.* Cambridge, MA: The MIT Press.

Spillane, J. P. (2004). *Standards deviation.* Cambridge, MA: Harvard University Press.

Stenner, A. J. (1996) *Measuring reading comprehension with the Lexile Framework.* Paper presented at the California Comparability Symposium, Burlingame, CA, October 31, 1996.

Stiggins, R. (2004). New assessment beliefs for a new school mission. *Phi Delta Kappan, 86*(1), 22 27.

Stigler, J., & Heibert, J. (1999). *The teaching gap.* New York: Free Press.

Stringfield, S., Ross, S., & Smith, L. (Eds.). (1996). *Bold plans for school restructuring: The New American Schools designs.* Mahwah, NJ: Lawrence Erlbaum.

Tharp, R. G., & Gallimore, R. (1988). *Rousing minds to life.* Cambridge, UK: Cambridge University Press.

Tomlinson, C. A. (1998). *The differentiated classroom: Responding to the needs of all learners.* Alexandria, VA: Association for Supervision and Curriculum Development.

Vygotsky, L. (1978). *Mind in society: The development of higher psychological processes* (M. Cole, V. John-Steiner, S. Scribner, & E. Souberman, Eds. & Trans.). Cambridge, MA: Harvard University Press.

Whitehurst, G. J. (2004). *Making education evidence-based: Premises, principles, pragmatics, and politics* (IPR Distinguished Public Policy Lecture Series 2003–04). Evanston, IL: Northwestern University, Institute for Policy Research.

Wilson, K. G., & Daviss, B. (1994). *Redesigning education.* New York: Henry Holt.

Wood, D. J., Bruner, J. S., & Ross, G. (1976). The role of tutoring in problem solving. *Journal of Child Psychology and Psychiatry, 17*(2), 89–100.

Index

Abrahamson, Eric, 14–15, 21
Accountability:
  advent of, school reform and, xii
  external, 7–8, 90
  internal, 6–8, 89, 90
Achievement, student, 9, 11, 12,
  31–32, 74, 92
Assessment:
  cycles of instruction and, 64
  for learning, 3, 18–20, 37,
    47–49, 92, 96–99
  formative, xiii, 10, 18–20, 33, 47
Assessment literacy, 92–93, 99
Assessment tools, 36, 48, 54,
  65–68, 80
Assisted development,
  theory of, 33

Black box, classroom instruction
  as, 29–30
Borman, G. D., 22–23
Breakthrough:
  achievement of, 13
  assessment for learning and, 20
  components of, 13–26. See also
    Breakthrough components
  defined, xi
  direct instruction vs., 11
  framework. See Breakthrough
    framework
  improved classroom
    instruction as, xv

personalization and, xvi
to transform classroom
  instruction, 35–38
Breakthrough components:
  personalization, 15–17
  precision, 15, 17–21
  professional learning, 15, 21–26
Breakthrough framework, 89–94
  core functions in, 91
  Triple P model in, 91
Building Essential Literacy (BEL),
  54, 84n3

Capacity building, 88, 93
Change, systemic, 89
Change knowledge, 87–89
Change Without Pain
  (Abrahamson), 14
Chicago, school reform studies in,
  3–8, 19–20, 24
Children's Literacy Success
  Strategy (CLaSS), 54, 84n3
Classroom, importance
  to Breakthrough
  leadership, 85
Classroom instruction:
  as "black box," 29–30
  best-practice, 28
  breakthrough to transform,
    35–38
  crux of problem, 31–33
  current model of, 29–31

day-to-day, professional
    development and, 86
dilemma of, 30–31
expert knowledge and, 46
learning theory basis of, 33–35
little change in, 41
making connections and, 34
reforms start with, 25
Classroom organization:
    Breakthrough framework
    and, 93
Classroom teaching strategies, 93.
    See also Teaching strategies
Clay, Marie, 78
CLIPs. *See* Critical Learning
    Instructional Paths
Cohen, D., 21–22, 24
Coherence:
    as precondition for reform, 27
    internal, 28
Comprehensive School Reform
    (CSR) designs, 9
Creative recombination, 14
Critical care paths, health care
    reform and, 52–54
Critical Learning Instructional
    Paths (CLIPs), 2, 54–55
    applied to early literacy,
        57–79
    applied to middle school
        math, 79
    components of system, 82–84
    data-driven instruction and,
        69–76
    implemented across many
        school systems, 81
    loops and detours in, 78–79
    mapping process for, 58–63
    measuring and monitoring
        learning, 63–69
    ongoing improvement and,
        80–81
Critical path, 52

Cross City Campaign for Urban
    School Reform, 3–8, 20, 24
Cycles of assessment and
    instruction, 64

Database, in CLIP, 82
Data Capture System, in
    CLIP, 83
Data-driven instruction, xvi, 2, 8,
    20, 69–76
Design:
    focus on improvement by,
        40–45
    use of term, 39
Design-based research, 43
Dewey, John, 41
DIBELS, 37, 66
Direct instruction, 9–11
District leadership, 96–97

Early literacy, stages of, 59–61
Education, current paradigm for,
    2–3
Educational research, natural
    sciences model, 43
Elmore, Richard, 6–8, 14, 21, 25,
    39, 42, 90, 98
England:
    Every Child Matters
        initiative, xvii
    literacy and numeracy
        initiative, 2
Expert instructional systems,
    45–47
    assessment for learning and,
        47–49
    CLIP and, 82–84
    critical learning instructional
        paths, 54–55
    establishing, 89
    focus on improvement by
        design, 40–45
    lessons from health care, 49–54

Expert systems, 46–47, 92
External accountability
    systems, 7–8

Feedback:
    as intervention, 10
    as key element of formative
        assessment, 18
    assessment for learning
        and, 19
    in Critical Learning
        Instructional Path,
        61–62
Flat performance, periods of, 7
Focused teaching:
    examples of, 34–35
    ingredients of, 36–38
    instructional programs for, 38
    student achievement and, 32–33
Focus Sheet, 69, 70, 74,
    75, 82, 84n3

Grade progression model, 31

Hargreaves, Andy, 9
Health care reform, 40–41
    critical care paths, 42–54
    lessons from, 49–54
Hill, H., 21–22, 24

Indicators of progress, 36, 61–63
Individualization, xvi. *See also*
    Personalization
Inference System, in CLIP, 82
Innovation, invention as, 13
Instruction:
    cycles of assessment and, 64
    defined, 29
    establishing starting points
        for, 63
    teaching vs., 29
Instructional path. *See* Critical
    Learning Instructional Paths

Instructional Strategies Matrix,
    72–74
Integrated care pathways, 52
Invention, as innovation, 13

Knowledge Base, in CLIP, 82

Leadership, system transformation
    and, 88
Learning:
    in context, 88
    measuring and monitoring,
        in CLIP, 63–69
    professional, 21–26, 86, 91
    relational, 86
Learning communities,
    professional, 21, 25,
    88, 93

Man: A Course of Study
    (MACOS), 41
Mapping process, 58–63
Mathematics, CLIP applied to
    middle school, 79–80
Mathematics reform, 21–22
Milwaukee, school reform studies
    in, 3–8, 20, 24
Moral purpose of education,
    12, 88, 92
Motivation, 32, 87

National Science Foundation
    (NSF), Urban Systemic
    Initiative, 22
Natural sciences model, 43
New American Schools
    Development
    corporation, 44
No Child Left Behind (NCLB),
    xvii, 88

Performance plateaus, 7
Performance Training Sects, 9

Personalization, xvi, 85
  as breakthrough component,
    15–17, 91
  focused teaching and, 38
  in health care, 49
Preassessment, 63
Precision, as breakthrough
    component, 15, 17–21, 91
Prescription, 8–12
Prescriptive teaching, 9.
    See also Direct instruction
Principal, role in Breakthrough
    leadership, 95–96
Professional development, 21
  day-to-day classroom
    practice and, 86
  disconnection between
    classroom experience
    and, 23
Professional learning,
    15, 21–26, 86, 91
Professional learning
    communities, 9, 21,
    25, 88, 93
Project Design Editor,
    in CLIP, 83

Record of reading, 67
Redesign process, 42
Reform. *See* School reform
Relational learning, 86
Research, educational, 43

Sadler, D. R., 18–19
School design:
  failure of, 44–45
  See also Design
School leadership, 95–96
School organization, 93
School reform:
  advent of accountability
    and, xii

coherence as precondition
    for, 27
  standards-based systemwide, 4
Schools:
  coherence between multiple
    levels of, 27
  default culture of public, xi
  new mission for. *See* New
    mission
School systems:
  CLIP implemented across
    many, 81
  new mission for, 1–12
Seattle, school reform studies in,
    3–8, 20, 24
Senge, P., 13–14, 16, 40
Simon, Herbert, 40
Six Drivers Model (NSF),
    22–23
Spillane, J., 86–87
State leadership, Breakthrough
    leadership and, 98–99
Student Learning Profile,
    71, 74
Success for All program, 11

Teaching:
  as art and science, 49
  expertise in, 47
  focused. *See* Focused
    teaching
  instruction vs., 29
  literacy, as time
    sensitive, 55
Teaching strategies:
  classroom, Breakthrough
    framework and, 93
  individual conferencing as
    effective, 76
Tipping point, xi, xv, 29
Tomlinson, Carol Ann,
    16, 77–78

Transformation, quick occurrence
    of, 28–29
Transformational Academic
    Achievement Planning
    Process (Seattle), 5
Tri-Level Reform Solution, 87–89
Triple P model, 91–92

Urban Systemic Initiative, 22
User Interface, with CLIP, 84

Vygotsky, L., 33

Zone of proximal development,
    33–35, 66

**CORWIN
PRESS**

The Corwin Press logo—a raven striding across an open book—represents the union of courage and learning. Corwin Press is committed to improving education for all learners by publishing books and other professional development resources for those serving the field of PreK–12 education. By providing practical, hands-on materials, Corwin Press continues to carry out the promise of its motto: **"Helping Educators Do Their Work Better."**

NSDC's mission is to ensure success for all students by serving as the international network for those who improve schools and by advancing individual and organization development.

The Ontario Principals' Council (OPC) is a voluntary professional association for principals and vice-principals in Ontario's public school system. We believe that exemplary leadership results in outstanding schools and improved student achievement. To this end, we foster quality leadership through world-class professional services and supports. As an ISO 9001 registered organization, we are committed to our statement that "quality leadership is our principal product."